BARRON'S BOOK NOTES

EDWARD ALBEE'S

Who's Afraid of Virginia Woolf?

D1638499

BARRON'S BOOK NOTES

EDWARD ALBEE'S
Who's Afraid of Virginia Woolf?

BY
Michael Adams

SERIES COORDINATOR
Murray Bromberg
Principal, Wang High School of Queens
Holliswood, New York
Past President
High School Principals Association of New York City

BARRON'S EDUCATIONAL SERIES, INC.
Woodbury, New York • London • Toronto • Sydney

All inquiries should be addressed to:
Barron's Educational Series, Inc.
113 Crossways Park Drive
Woodbury, New York 11797

Library of Congress Catalog Card No. 85-3963

International Standard Book No. 0-7641-9131-4

Library of Congress Cataloging in Publication Data
Adams, Michael, 1947 Aug. 14–
    Edward Albee's Who's Afraid of Virginia Woolf?

    (Barron's book notes)
    Bibliography: p.107
    Summary: A guide to reading "Who's Afraid of
Virginia Woolf?" with a critical and appreciative mind
encouraging analysis of plot, style, form, and
structure. Also includes background on the author's
life and time, sample tests, term paper suggestions,
and a reading list.
    1. Albee, Edward, 1928–   . Who's afraid of
Virginia Woolf? [1. Albee, Edward, 1928–   . Who's
afraid of Virginia Woolf? 2. American literature—
History and criticism] I. Title. II. Series.
PS3551.L25W432 1985   812'.54   85-3963
ISBN 0-7641-9131-4

PRINTED IN THE UNITED STATES OF AMERICA

567   550   987654321

CONTENTS

ADVISORY BOARD

We wish to thank the following educators who helped us focus our *Book Notes* series to meet student needs and critiqued our manuscripts to provide quality materials.

Sandra Dunn, English Teacher
Hempstead High School, Hempstead, New York

Lawrence J. Epstein, Associate Professor of English
Suffolk County Community College, Selden, New York

Leonard Gardner, Lecturer, English Department
State University of New York at Stony Brook

Beverly A. Haley, Member, Advisory Committee
National Council of Teachers of English Student
Guide Series, Fort Morgan, Colorado

Elaine C. Johnson, English Teacher
Tamalpais Union High School District
Mill Valley, California

Marvin J. LaHood, Professor of English
State University of New York College at Buffalo

Robert Lecker, Associate Professor of English
McGill University, Montréal, Québec, Canada

David E. Manly, Professor of Educational Studies
State University of New York College at Geneseo

Bruce Miller, Associate Professor of Education
State University of New York at Buffalo

Frank O'Hare, Professor of English and
Director of Writing
Ohio State University, Columbus, Ohio

Faith Z. Schullstrom, Member, Executive Committee
National Council of Teachers of English
Director of Curriculum and Instruction
Guilderland Central School District, New York

Mattie C. Williams, Director, Bureau of Language Arts
Chicago Public Schools, Chicago, Illinois

HOW TO USE THIS BOOK

You have to know how to approach literature in order to get the most out of it. This *Barron's Book Notes* volume follows a plan based on methods used by some of the best students to read a work of literature.

Begin with the guide's section on the author's life and times. As you read, try to form a clear picture of the author's personality, circumstances, and motives for writing the work. This background usually will make it easier for you to hear the author's tone of voice, and follow where the author is heading.

Then go over the rest of the introductory material—such sections as those on the plot, characters, setting, themes, and style of the work. Underline, or write down in your notebook, particular things to watch for, such as contrasts between characters and repeated literary devices. At this point, you may want to develop a system of symbols to use in marking your text as you read. (Of course, you should only mark up a book you own, not one that belongs to another person or a school.) Perhaps you will want to use a different letter for each character's name, a different number for each major theme of the book, a different color for each important symbol or literary device. Be prepared to mark up the pages of your book as you read. Put your marks in the margins so you can find them again easily.

Now comes the moment you've been waiting for—the time to start reading the work of literature. You may want to put aside your *Barron's Book Notes* volume until you've read the work all the way through. Or you may want to alternate, reading the *Book Notes* analysis of each section as soon as you have finished reading the corresponding part of the original. Before you move on, reread crucial passages you don't fully understand. (Don't take this guide's analysis for granted—make up your own mind as to what the work means.)

Once you've finished the whole work of literature, you may want to review it right away, so you can firm up your ideas about what it means. You may want to leaf through the book concentrating on passages you marked in reference to one character or one theme. This is also a good time to reread the *Book Notes* introductory material, which pulls together insights on specific topics.

When it comes time to prepare for a test or to write a paper, you'll already have formed ideas about the work. You'll be able to go back through it, refreshing your memory as to the author's exact words and perspective, so that you can support your opinions with evidence drawn straight from the work. Patterns will emerge, and ideas will fall into place; your essay question or term paper will almost write itself. Give yourself a dry run with one of the sample tests in the guide. These tests present both multiple-choice and essay questions. An accompanying section gives answers to the multiple-choice questions as well as suggestions for writing the essays. If you have to select a term paper topic, you may choose one from the list of suggestions in this book. This guide also provides you with a reading list, to help you when you start research for a term paper, and a selection of provocative comments by critics, to spark your thinking before you write.

THE AUTHOR
AND HIS TIMES

In 1962 the United States was enjoying what many now consider a period of innocence. John F. Kennedy, the youngest man ever elected President, was in office, revitalizing a country some observers considered passive and complacent when he was inaugurated in 1961. Relative peace reigned in most of the world, and in the United States traditional values appeared unshakable. Hardly anyone would have predicted the great turmoil the country was about to undergo—the Vietnam War; the assassinations of President Kennedy, Senator Robert F. Kennedy, and Reverend Martin Luther King, Jr.; and the scandal of Watergate that led to the resignation of President Richard M. Nixon in 1974.

Yet, if the surface was tranquil in 1962, there was nonetheless considerable agitation underneath. American relations with the Soviet Union were often extremely tense in the early 1960s, resulting in confrontations over Berlin and Cuba. In the United States, attempts by blacks to end racial discrimination not infrequently were countered by violence by whites. And a number of influential writers were questioning the American values that seemed so secure.

On October 13, 1962, a play opened on Broadway in New York City that was one of the first popular successes to articulate these undercurrents of dissatisfaction, of unease about America.

That play, Edward Albee's *Who's Afraid of Virginia Woolf?*, critically analyzed institutions and values that Americans held dear—family, marriage, and success, for instance—and suggested they might have been created in part to escape from reality.

Albee's play set loose a cyclone of controversy. It was the rare case of a play created for the commercial theater presenting a full-scale investigation of sacred American traditions, and it did so in shocking language that many found disturbing.

Yet for every person who found *Who's Afraid of Virginia Woolf?* "perverse" and "dirty-minded," there were those who labeled the play a masterpiece and declared Albee to be "one of the most important dramatists of the contemporary world theater." Debate raged over the play, and opinions were even offered by people who had never seen or read it!

Who *is* the man who nearly turned the theater world upside down in 1962? It's not an easy question to answer, since Edward Albee always has been an intensely private man. Anyone who looks to Albee's life for hints about his work probably will be disappointed, for few modern writers have been so guarded about their past and protective of their privacy. In a 1981 interview Albee was asked how important his biography was as a key to understanding his work. He responded: "I think totally unimportant. I'd rather people judge the work for itself rather than by biographical attachments."

You may not agree with Albee about how much your knowledge of an author's life helps you understand his work, but Albee's philosophy of allowing the work to speak for itself deserves respect.

The facts known about Albee's early life come from the information he has made public, plus the reminiscences of longtime friends. Albee was born in Washington, D.C., on March 12, 1928, to parents whose identities are unknown. He was placed in an orphanage at birth, and at the age of two weeks he was adopted by Reed and Frances Albee, who took him to live in New York City. He was named Edward Franklin Albee after a grandfather, who was part owner of the Keith-Albee Circuit, an extremely successful string of vaudeville theaters.

The Albee family was wealthy, and young Edward's life was one of luxury. His childhood included private tutors, servants, luxury automobiles, winters in warm climates, excursions to the theater, and riding lessons. But such privilege as a child did not result in a pampered complacency when he grew up. In fact, as you shall see, Albee used his pen to criticize the moral and spiritual damage inflicted upon people by an excess of material wealth and a misguided pursuit of the "American dream."

The family moved around a lot, and this may have created problems for Albee's education. He attended a variety of schools and was expelled from both a preparatory school and a military academy. He graduated from Choate, a fashionable private school in Connecticut, however. He then enrolled at Trinity College, also in Connecticut, but left after his sophomore year to begin a life on his own in New York City's Greenwich Village.

Greenwich Village in 1950 was a haven for young writers and bohemians looking for artistic freedom and inspiration. Albee's search for independence was helped greatly by a trust fund set up for him by his grandmother. Despite the steady income (which earned him the title "the richest boy in Greenwich Village" from his friends), Albee took a variety of odd jobs: office boy, record and book salesman, writer of radio and music programs, and Western Union messenger. Some say he delivered death notices for the telegraph company, an interesting item to remember as you read *Who's Afraid of Virginia Woolf?*

Although it has been suggested that Albee lived a rebellious and restless existence during the 1950s, some say his life was stable and comfortable. Two facts are verifiable: he loved the theater and he loved to write. (His first play, *Aliqueen*, was written when he was twelve.)

Just before his thirtieth birthday in 1958, after a period of unsuccessful writing, Albee wrote *The Zoo Story*. It was a one-act play that would eventually win him worldwide attention. Through friends, Albee had the play produced first in West Berlin, and then in twelve West German cities, where the theatrical climate was more experimental than in the United States. Thus, Albee saw *The Zoo Story* produced first in a language he didn't understand!

The Zoo Story premiered in New York in 1960 at an off-Broadway theater. Word quickly spread that a writer of great promise had appeared on the scene. Albee's reputation among knowledgeable theatergoers grew with other one-acters: *The Death of Bessie Smith*, *The Sandbox*, and *The American Dream*.

Albee's explosion on the theatrical scene came at a time when the American commercial theater had been dominated by playwrights such as Arthur Miller, Tennessee Williams, and William Inge.

These writers worked for the most part in a realistic idiom, in which the world onstage essentially mirrored the world of the audience. The world was observed objectively, and in ways that generally echoed traditional values and supported the beliefs of the audience. These plays told the members of the audience that men and women were basically reponsible for determining their own fate.

Some playwrights of the time, particularly Europeans like Samuel Beckett, Jean Genet, and Eugene Ionesco, were responding differently to the world. World War II and the potential horrors of the nuclear age compelled these writers to see the universe as a place where humans had lost control. They were eager to shake audiences out of a sense of complacency about their lives. They wanted the spectator to feel their deep-seated anguish at the absurdity of the human condition. Nothing happens, nothing changes, these writers say. The world is out of control and nothing we can do will change this disturbing condition. This attitude of hopelessness prompted the critics to loosely categorize these writers as Absurdists.

Plays of the Theater of the Absurd, such as Beckett's *Waiting for Godot* (1953) and *Endgame* (1957) and Ionesco's *The Bald Soprano* (1950), share certain characteristics. Speech is often deliberately confusing and not logical. The patter is filled with jargon, clichés, even nonsense, as if to tell us that language itself is empty and our attempts to communicate deep feelings are futile. Dramatic and realistic characters are frequently eliminated. The plays are often merely a series or incidents or images that represent the turmoil of the human condition as the author sees it. Also, absurdist plays are often very funny—sometimes insanely so—suggesting that laughter is the only response to the pain of life in a world devoid of hope or purpose.

Albee's work includes both realisitc and absurdist techniques. He is often seen as a link between these two movements. On one level, *The Zoo Story* tells of an "ordinary" meeting between two men in a park. Peter is a comfortable middle-class businessman, the upholder of traditional American values, complete with wife, children, and pets. Jerry is an outcast and a rebel, a man who has chosen to remove himself from the mainstream by living a solitary, introspective existence. The play concerns Jerry's desire to communicate with Peter on something more than a superficial level, and when his initial attempts fail, he compels Peter to murder him, suggesting that only violence or death can bring communication at a deeper level. The themes of communication through violence and the hollowness of American values that Albee explores in *The Zoo Story* link him with the absurdists, as does Jerry's death, which has been likened to the death of the student in Ionesco's play *The Lesson*. (These two themes and a death surface again in *Who's Afraid of Virginia Woolf?*)

The Sandbox (1959) and *The American Dream* (1960) are short plays by Albee that deal with the same three characters: Mommy, dominating and cruel; Daddy, passive and emasculated; and Grandma, shrewd and sharp-tongued. In *The Sandbox*, Death comes to Grandma on the beach in the form of a handsome young man, while Mommy and Daddy bicker endlessly. *The American Dream* shows the family at home as they are visited by the identical twin of a child they had once adopted and then destroyed. With exaggeration and bitter parody, Albee reveals "the American Dream"—the seemingly perfect nuclear family whose polished exterior conceals cruelty, dishonesty, and hatred.

Who's Afraid of Virginia Woolf? explores themes—death, sterility, the corruption of the American dream—similar to Albee's earlier one-act plays. In some ways this full-length play is more realistic than its predecessors. It has a recognizable setting and more commonplace characters. But the absurdist influence is there too—in the imaginary child that George and Martha have created in the characters' inability to communicate except through abrasiveness and violence, and in the frequent use of clichéd speech. It is the successful blending of realism and absurdism that has prompted audiences to applaud Albee's innovations. Yet some readers feel that the play would be better served by a nonrealistic production, perhaps a blank stage rather than the detailed setting it's usually given.

The controversy generated by the play's Broadway opening reached a climax with the awarding of the Pulitzer Prize for Drama, one of the most prestigious of all drama awards. The committee chosen to select the winning play voted to give the prize to *Who's Afraid of Virginia Woolf?*, but the trustees of Columbia University, the overseers of the award, decided to deny the play a Pulitzer. They perhaps felt that its explicit language and its exploration of "taboo" subjects made it too controversial a choice.

Despite its detractors, the play has continued to be performed, debated, and admired. (A successful film version starred the popular actors Richard

Burton and Elizabeth Taylor; Taylor won an Academy Award in 1966 for her portrayal of Martha.) In the seventies, there was a major Broadway revival of the play with Colleen Dewhurst and Ben Gazzara. If it has been revived less than other major plays, it may be that audiences have grown accustomed to its troubled message in an age of cynicism and nihilism. Also, the heavy demands made by the play on its cast (particularly on the actors playing George and Martha) discourage many theater companies from including it in their repertory.

Yet for those who can't see a production of the play, the text can provide an opportunity to study Albee's characters and language more fully. The elements of the play that were once so shocking—perhaps even offensive—seem almost tame in an era of sexual permissiveness on stage, screen and television. That the play continues to generate enormous power suggests to many playgoers and readers that Albee has indeed created an enduring masterpiece.

After *Virginia Woolf*, Albee continued to experiment. His next play, *Tiny Alice* (1964), is a dark and mysterious allegory about man's relationship to God. In 1966 he won the Pulitzer Prize for *A Delicate Balance*, which tells of a "conventional" family whose lives are overturned when good friends invade their household, driven from their own home by a nameless fear. *All Over* (1971) details the reactions of a group of people—relatives and loved ones—to the death of a famous writer. *Box* and *Quotations from Chairman Mao Tse-Tung* (1968) are two interrelated one-acters. In *Box* there are no characters; a box sits on stage and a voice from within it speaks to the audience. In *Seascape*

(1975), which also won a Pulitzer Prize, two of the four characters are large lizardlike creatures that emerge from the sea.

Among Albee's other works are adaptations of novels, which audiences and readers have never felt to be among his best work: Carson McCullers' *Ballad of the Sad Cafe* (1963), James Purdy's *Malcolm* (1965), and Vladimir Nabokov's *Lolita* (1981). Albee has even written a musical, an adaptation of Truman Capote's short novel, *Breakfast at Tiffany's*, which closed before it got to Broadway.

By the mid-1980s none of Albee's other plays had received the critical acclaim or popular acceptance of *Who's Afraid of Virginia Woolf?* Some people felt that his plays had become more and more inaccessible, that Albee was speaking to himself in his own coded language, with little regard for how well he communicated with the audience. Others defended him by saying that his lack of interest in the commercial theater should not be held against him, and that perhaps the test of time would prove his later works to be among his best.

What was important was that Albee, who had long disregarded the opinion of critics ("I have been both overpraised and underpraised," he had said), kept writing. He was not content to rest on past laurels. He also gave generously of his time and energy to other artists, both as a founder of the William Flanagan Center for Creative Persons, at Montauk, New York, and as a member of national and state organizations furthering the arts. Although reluctant to talk about his life or his past, Albee was dedicated to artistic excellence and often shared his expertise with college students in lectures and seminars.

It was also clear that he had a major influence

on his younger contemporaries. Evidence of his remarkable ear for dialogue, his poetic flair for the American idiom, and his cynical viewpoint on American values could be seen in the work of such playwrights as Sam Shephard (*Buried Child, True West, Fool for Love*), David Rabe (*Streamers, Hurlyburly*); John Guare (*House of Blue Leaves*); and David Mamet (*American Buffalo, Glengarry Glen Ross*).

THE PLAY

The Plot

Late one Saturday night, a husband and wife return to their home in a New England college town. George, 46, is an associate professor of history; Martha, 52, is the daughter of the college president. They have been drinking heavily at a faculty party given by Martha's father, and as the two stumble around the living room and bicker, they seem like many other such couples after a long and alcoholic party. But this is a night in which tensions within their marriage will erupt and the patterns of their lives may be altered forever.

To George's surprise, Martha announces that she has invited another couple to join them for a drink— at 2 A.M.! Naturally combative, George and Martha use the invitation as another excuse to battle.

The guests arrive—Nick, 30, a new faculty member in the biology department, and his wife, Honey 26. He's good-looking and athletic; she's a sweet and seemingly superficial person. They quickly find themselves to be the audience for George and Martha's scalding war of words.

As the evening progresses and the liquor flows, tensions that have been partially hidden emerge in the form of psychological games. Martha is disgusted with George's lack of ambition and failure to advance in the history department, particularly with his advantages as the son-in-law of the university president. She treats George with open contempt, and George tries to strike back by using

his superior verbal skills. He has taken an immediate dislike to Nick, not only because Martha is
obviously physically attracted to the younger man,
but also because Nick is a biologist. As a historian,
George sees biology as a science determined to
eliminate man's individuality.

Nick tries to stay detached from the turmoil between his hosts, but he soon gets caught up in it
and reveals himself as ambitious and shallow.
Honey seems too drunk and too mindless to com-
prehend much of what is going on.

A turning point occurs when George discovers
that Martha has mentioned a forbidden topic to
Honey while the two women were out of the room.
The taboo topic: George and Martha's son. The
bitterness between the couple accelerates, and they
persist in their battle of verbal abuse. As Act I ends,
Martha has figuratively twisted a knife in George's
back by harping on his supposed failure as a man
and as a teacher. The fight dissolves into a shouting
match and Honey is made physically ill by a combination of the quarreling and too much alcohol.

As Act II of the play opens, George and Nick
talk alone. George tells the story of a young boy
who killed his mother and caused his father to die,
a story that may or may not be autobiographical.
Nick reveals that he married Honey when she
thought she was pregnant, but that the pregnancy
turned out to be a false alarm. George's attempts
to warn Nick about being "dragged down by the
quicksand" of the college fall on deaf ears. Nick
has his eye set on the top, and one of his techniques for advancement will be to sleep with a few
important faculty wives.

Martha and Honey return, and the sexual attraction between Martha and Nick increases. They dance erotically with each other as Martha goads her husband by telling their guests of George's attempts to write a novel, whose plot concerns a boy responsible for his parents' deaths. Infuriated, George physically attacks Martha, stopping only when Nick intervenes. George seeks his revenge, not on Martha, but on the guests. He tells a "fable" that mirrors Nick and Honey's early lives and her hysterical pregnancy. Humiliated, Honey flees the room. Enraged and out for blood, George and Martha declare "total war" on each other.

The first victory is Martha's, as she openly makes sexual advances to Nick but fails to make George lose his temper. Yet after she has led the younger man to the kitchen, where George can hear the sounds of their carousing, George makes a decision that will be his final act of revenge, one that will change his and Martha's lives forever: he decides to tell her that their son is dead.

Act III finds Martha alone. Nick has proven himself impotent in their sexual encounter, and when he arrives again on the scene, she expresses contempt for him. She also reveals to him that George is the only man who has ever satisfied her.

George appears at the front door, bearing flowers and announcing that there is one more game to play—"Bringing Up Baby." First, he induces Martha to talk about their son in the most loving and idealized terms; then, he announces the death of their son.

Martha's furious reaction that George "cannot decide these things" leads Nick to understand at last George and Martha's secret. Their son is a creation of their imagination, a fantasy child that they have carefully harbored as a means of helping them survive the pain of their failed lives. Nick and Honey leave, and George and Martha are alone, with just each other as shields against the world. Only the future will tell whether thay have been strengthened or made even more vulnerable by the traumatic experiences of the evening.

The Characters

George

George is an associate professor of history at a college in the New England town of New Carthage. At 46, he should probably be further along in his career, but through a lack of ambition, coupled with a bad relationship with the college president (his father-in-law), he has become "bogged down" in the history department. He's been married to Martha, six years older than he, for 23 years, and their marriage has degenerated into an ongoing battle of words and psychological games to get the upper hand.

George is intelligent and witty, and has a keen ability to use words. In fact, he might be an excellent dinner companion if his basic energy had not been dissipated by Martha's constant belittling of him. He fights back by using his wits, but she knows where to wound him at his most vulnerable points—his failures, his physical weakness, his passivity.

Virtually nothing is told us of George's (or the other characters') early life. George relates a story that he claims to be autobiographical, about a trip to a gin mill (saloon) during the Prohibition era, when he was a teenager. But there are clues to

suggest that a boy in the story whom George refers to as a "friend" may actually be George himself. This boy had murdered his mother and
caused the death of his father. Whether the story
is literal or metaphoric is never made clear in the
play, nor is it known if George is talking about
himself or someone else. Whatever interpretation
is accepted, however, it's evident that George
suffers from a great deal of conflict about his parents, and seems to harbor guilt and/or resent-
ment about them.

Through most of the play Martha gets the better
of George, beating him down psychologically. She
is skillful at dishing out punishment, and George
accepts it. He turns the tables by abusing their
guests in ways similar to Martha's treatment of
him, by chiding them for their weaknesses and
revealing their hidden secrets.

In the end, however, George proves himself
stronger than Martha. His decision to kill their
imaginary child—a fantasy he and Martha have
shared privately—can be viewed as an act of hero-
ism or as an act of revenge. Whichever approach
you favor, it is clear that George is in control by
the end of the play.

To some readers, George's name suggests
George Washington (an ironic comment on the
corruption of American ideals); to others, it suggests St. George, the dragon slayer who conquered evil (much as George conquers the "devil"
that possesses him and his wife in the form of
the child fantasy).

Martha
Martha is the daughter of the college president,
and one of the great conflicts of her life is that

while she reveres her father, he seems to have no great love for her.

Intelligent, well-read, and perceptive, Martha hides her intellectual gifts beneath a brassy, aggressive, and vulgar exterior. She tries to dominate and control her husband for two reasons: she resents his inability to fill her father's role, both professionally and psychologically; and George seems to enjoy the role of victim to her torturer.

Martha battles almost continuously with George as an act of attempted communication. Faced with lives filled with self-loathing, they punish each other at the same time they wish to connect. Both drink heavily, and Martha seduces a number of younger men. A self-styled "earth mother," Martha admits that these encounters are unsatisfying; the only man who has given her true satisfaction is George. But it's one of the tragic ironies of the play that their mutual need can never be expressed to each other.

Only when George successfully ends their fantasy of having a child does Martha admit a vulnerability and a fear of the future that she has not revealed before, but what lies ahead for her and George remains ambiguous.

Like George, Martha's name is perhaps meant to evoke Martha Washington, the wife of George Washington. Together they can be seen as offering a wry commentary on the "perfect American couple."

Nick

One of George and Martha's guests, Nick is young (30), attractive, and physically fit. A biology professor, new to the faculty, Nick seems the ideal man, but he eventually reveals himself to have a hollow center. He is amoral, shallow, coldly ambitious. His plans to get ahead at the college include sleeping with "pertinent" faculty wives.

His willingness to be seduced by Martha, despite the presence of his wife and George, is evidence of his cynicism and lack of morals. But underneath the macho exterior is a weak and crass human being. He is impotent in his sexual encounter with Martha, and he admits to having married Honey because he thought she was pregnant and because her father was wealthy.

Nick's profession as a biologist is contrasted to George's as a historian. Biology in the play is viewed as the science whose practitioners are determined to toy with human genetics in order to create a race of perfect human beings. Nick therefore suggests the results of these experiments, the "wave of the future"—attractive on the outside, empty within.

Nick is the one character who comes to understand that George and Martha's son is an imaginary creation, and his half hearted attempt to help ("I'd like to . . . ") suggests to some that the evening spent with George and Martha has changed him. But Albee gives no further clues as to what the future holds for Nick and Honey.

Nick's name may suggest an old-fashioned term for the devil ("Old Nick"). Whether he's meant to represent a literal evil that invades George and Martha's household, or perhaps the evil of the future, is open to debate. Some readers believe his name refers to Nikita Khrushchev, the premier of the Soviet Union at the time the play was written. Thus, Nick's confrontations with George may suggest East vs. West, the energetic threat of Communism in contrast to decaying American ideals.

Honey

Nick's wife, Honey, 26, is, on the surface, sweet, gentle, eager to make a good impression, and prudish. She is also unable to handle her liquor, so her contributions to the conversation are minor at best. Her mindlessness turns out to reveal an inability to cope with reality.

Honey shows herself on one level to be the eternal child. She defers to her husband, is easily offended, gives in to frequent bouts of vomiting. Yet, in the course of the play she also reveals complex emotions. The daughter of a moderately famous preacher who left her a sizable amount of money, Honey was apparently pregnant when she married Nick, but the pregnancy turned out to be a false alarm. Since then she has skillfully concealed from Nick her efforts to prevent a pregnancy. Her use of secret birth control devices reveals a deep-seated fear of having a child—and a fear of growing up. Martha's beautiful descriptions of her own "son" bring out Honey's maternal instincts, but whether these desires are fleeting or permanent cannot be determined within the context of the play.

Honey's name suggests the cloying sweetness that is her exterior—and also the sense that a little of her goes a long way. Some readers feel that "Honey" is not her real name, but merely the affectionate and condescending tag Nick has given her.

Other Elements

SETTING

Who's Afraid of Virginia Woolf? is set in the fictitious New England college town of New Carthage. The name of the town suggests the ancient civilization of Carthage, which for nearly
1,500 years (from the 8th century B.C. to the 7th
century A.D.) was the most important settlement
west of Egypt on the northern coast of Africa.
Carthage was settled by the Phoenicians, a people known for their seafaring and commerce, in
the 9th century B.C. Over the next several centuries, Carthage was able to hold its own in battles
with Greece, but a series of conflicts with Rome
in the third and second centuries B.C., known as
the Punic Wars, proved to be the downfall of the
Carthaginians. The Romans permanently conquered Carthage in 146 B.C. and, as was their
custom, sowed the vanquished's land with salt,
to prevent fertile growth for years to come.

Albee's decision to name the play's college town
after a vanished civilization (which was known for
its artistic achievement as well as its military power)
clearly invites parallels to our own contemporary
civilization. America may not be destroyed by another country, as Carthage was (although that possibility exists), but it may meet its downfall through
internal corruption and spiritual emptiness. That
Carthage was made literally sterile by Roman salt
also links that ancient city symbolically with New
Carthage, a city made figuratively sterile by shoddy
morals and hollow values. (New Carthage also is

the home of George and Martha, sterile because
they can have no children.)

Placing New Carthage in New England ironically links the setting of the play to one of its themes,
"American values." New England was a birthplace
of America's freedom and has long been considered a stronghold of solid American values. By setting a play that analyzes the corruption of some of
these values in an area long identified with them,
Albee emphasizes the difference between what
these values were and what they have become.

Further irony is to be found in Albee's choice of
an academic setting for the play. One would think
that a college town would be a place of learning,
achievement, and sophisticated culture. Instead,
Albee shows us a hotbed of lust, deception, and
sadness, with people who are motivated in large
part by greed and self-interest.

Confining the play's setting to one room (the
living room of George and Martha) establishes an
enclosed, claustrophobic feeling, as if the characters are trapped with each other. Even when they
leave to go to another room, they return to this
arena where the battles of the play rage.

When *Who's Afraid of Virginia Woolf?* was origi-
nally produced on Broadway, the set was de-
scribed by the play's director, Alan Schneider, as
follows: "It seems real . . . but it's not real. It has
all kinds of angles and planes that you wouldn't
ordinarily have, and strong distortions." Schneider said, and others have agreed, that the play
could be done on an abstract (nonrealistic) set, such
as an all-white space. Such a set would heighten
the sense that the play is not strictly realistic, but
has overtones of the Theater of the Absurd.

THEMES

Here are some of the major and minor themes of *Who's Afraid of Virginia Woolf?* The themes often overlap and support one another in ways that make the play complex and richly textured.

Major Themes

1. TRUTH AND ILLUSION

Both George and Martha state this theme explicitly in Act III, as the line between the real and the imaginary begins to blur, particularly for Martha. Their marriage, possibly their lives, has been held together by an illusion—the imaginary child that they have created together and that must now be "destroyed" if they are to face reality. Admitting this illusion to themselves and to Nick and Honey calls into question other things George and Martha say in the play. For example, did George really cause the death of his parents, or is this, too, a myth that has become real for them?

Other elements underscore the theme: Honey's imaginary pregnancy; the shotgun that turns out to be a toy; the chimes accidentally struck, that George uses to herald the pretended arrival of the telegram. Throughout the play the characters use many devices to keep from facing the real world: alcohol, sex, and constant verbal assaults on one another.

Also, the surface "truth" of the characters masks their real selves; the characters are not what they seem. The brash and vulgar Martha is truly vulnerable, the one who may need the most protection from the real world. George, seemingly passive and dominated, is the one who finally takes control of his and Martha's lives. Nick, an apparent "stud," turns out to be impotent in bed with Martha. And Honey, the seemingly simple and ingenuous personality, has been deviously using birth control to prevent a pregnancy.

This is the play's most important theme: that people today have been forced to create illusions for themselves because reality has become too difficult and too painful to face. What examples do you see of the need for illusion in your own life or in the lives of those around you?

2. THE INABILITY TO COMMUNICATE

The characters are constantly, but unsuccessfully, attempting to communicate on a deeper level with each other. Martha and George trade competitive insults and verbal cruelties until the last scene, when they finally achieve some sense of mutual understanding.

Yet their attempts to communicate seem more genuine than those of Nick and Honey, who seem to know each other only superficially and who deliberately deceive each other—Nick with his adulterous act with Martha, and Honey with her secret use of birth control.

The usual social communication is parodied throughout the play through the use of trite remarks and common phrases that suggest the emptiness of language. Early in the play, George seems determined to confuse Nick with wordplay, rapid shifts of subject, and deliberate obtuseness.

Violence as a form of communication is demonstrated through the tale of George and Martha's boxing match, his fake rifle, and the physical scuffles between George and Martha. Psychological violence as a form of communication is evidenced by George and Martha's repeated attempts to humiliate each other, and by George's decision to "get the guests."

In this media age, the word *communication* is heard often. Is Martha and George's problem in truly reaching each other a universal problem? In what ways do you see the problem affecting those around you?

3. SEX (STERILITY AND IMPOTENCE)

Sex is a strong motif in the play. Martha is a sexually aggressive "earth mother," who presumably seduced the gardener at her boarding school and also "attacked" a Greek artist. George even accuses her of having tried to molest their imaginary son. And Martha's seduction of Nick during the play is probably one of many such escapades. There is a great deal of sexual innuendo among the four characters.

Honey, Nick, and Martha all seem to be sexual "users." Honey may have used a false pregnancy to get Nick to marry her. Nick hints of plans to sleep with important faculty wives to get ahead at the college. Martha uses sex with others to get even with George, whom she blames for her unhappiness.

However, sex in the play represents barrenness and impotence. George and Martha's child is imaginary, Honey's pregnancy was false and she fears childbirth, and Nick can't satisfy Martha, the most important faculty wife. Even the name of the town, New Carthage, suggests the ancient civilization destroyed by Rome and sown with salt to prevent fertile growth. In the world of this play, sex is neither a comfort nor a source of growth.

4. GAMES AND GAMESMANSHIP

Games, both literal and figurative, abound in the play. Several are mentioned explicitly: humiliate the host, hump the hostess, get the guest, bringing up baby.

There are also abundant references to games, rules, toys, winners and losers. George and Martha are constantly playing games, matching wits, seeking the upper hand. And the scenes between George and Nick have been compared to a chess match, with each player seeking the advantage over the other.

The ultimate game in the play is George and Martha's child, an invention of their imagination that must be destroyed now that Martha has broken the rules by mentioning him. The child is a game that is deadly serious. When the game is over, the future of George and Martha is in question.

5. MARRIAGE AND FAMILY RELATIONSHIPS

The couples in the play can be seen as representative of modern relationships based on deception and sterility, and the picture of the play presents of marriage is bleak. George and Martha face off in a "battle of the sexes" that is an age-old theme in plays, from Aristophanes' *Lysistrata*, to Shakespeare's *Much Ado About Nothing* and *The Taming of the Shrew*, and to Noel Coward's *Private Lives*. But unlike many such plays, *Who's Afraid of Virginia Woolf?* shows characters who are out for blood.

George and Martha hide their need for each other with ferocious assaults on one another. Their names suggest the "first couple," George and Martha Washington, a grim joke that underscores the corruption of the American ideal. But their fierce battling may be seen as preferable to the shallowness that marks the relationship between Nick and Honey.

The family relationships referred to in the play are hollow and sad: Martha and her father, George and the parents he might have killed, Honey and her father, and George and Martha's "child."

Sterility is evidenced by the play's use of imaginary and would-be children: George and Martha's fictitious boy and the pregnancies that Honey has deviously avoided. As an ironic twist, Albee has peppered the play with allusions to "baby": George and Martha use the term as a dubious endearment; they also use coy baby talk; Honey becomes a baby, curled on the bathroom floor in the fetal position as a sign of her inability to grow up.

Some readers, however, see the play's depiction of George and Martha in a more optimistic light. They interpret the play as the story of one couple's desperate attempt to salvage, rather than destroy, a relationship. After the evening's emotional turmoil, notably the "death" of the child, George and Martha have cleared up some of the matters impeding the relationship, and they may be able to function better as a couple in the future.

Minor Themes
1. DEATH AND MURDER
The theme of death pervades the play. George and Martha's son is killed symbolically by exor-

cism (as George reads from the mass for the dead).
George himself may have murdered his mother
and caused his father's death. Threats to kill and
accusations of murder occur several times in the
play.

2. RELIGION

References to God and Jesus (often used as swear
words) are frequent, forming an almost subconscious thematic element. Other religious references are more apparent. Martha declares herself
an atheist. The second act title "Walpurgisnacht,"
refers to a pagan ritual. The third act title, "The
Exorcism," is taken from the Catholic rite of driving out demons. George recites the *Dies Irae*, the
mass for the dead, as Martha is forced to accept
the death of their son.

Some readers feel that Albee used the name
"Nick," part of an old term for the devil ("Old
Nick") to suggest that it is Nick's presence that
brings chaos to George and Martha's lives. Others
see significance in the fact that the play takes place
very early on a Sunday morning, a day of holiness
for Christians.

Does this abundance of religious symbols and
allusions suggest a possibility of redemption for
George and Martha? Some say yes. Others suggest
that there is no hope for them, and that Albee is
pointing a finger at the failure of modern religion to
supply answers to the problems of people today.

3. HISTORY VS. SCIENCE

George is a history professor; Nick teaches biology. George's work concerns the endless variety
of human motivation and endeavor, while Nick's

work—according to George—will result in the "perfect man," a creation with no need for art, philosophy, diversity, or real pleasure. Since Albee gives the eloquent speeches to George, it has been suggested that Albee is using George's character to condemn science for many of the ills of mankind.

4. AMERICAN VALUES

Albee painstakingly dissects the "American dream" in many of his plays; he even gave one of his early one-act plays that title. In *Who's Afraid of Virginia Woolf?* he attacks many of the values that traditionally comprise that dream: marriage, children, success, wealth, education, religion, and so on. He claims each of these values to be empty, resulting in loveless and sterile marriages, failed careers, ill-gotten wealth, squandered education, powerless or corrupt religion. With these values so decayed, Albee seems to be saying, the country is a barren wasteland, where people must imagine another reality in order to compensate for what is missing. In *Virginia Woolf*, Albee has painted a bleak and unflattering portrait of a country whose ideals have degenerated so fully that they can be portrayed by a desperate, sad, and seemingly hopeless couple.

STYLE

Soon after *Who's Afraid of Virginia Woolf?* opened on Broadway, Harold Clurman, a noted theater critic, wrote the following about Albee's dialogue: "It is superbly virile and pliant; it also *sounds*. It is not 'realistic' dialogue, but a highly literate and full-bodied distillation of common American speech."

Clurman is not alone in his admiration for Albee's dialogue. Even those who found the play's themes too unsettling or the subject matter unsavory had high praise for his skill as a playwright.

His sharp and incisive dialogue is only one of the elements that make Albee's style both recognizable and memorable. Here are some others:

Humor For all of the play's savagery and bleak outlook, *Who's Afraid of Virginia Woolf?* is often very funny. George and Martha are so verbally skillful that their exchanges often make you laugh at the same time you feel the pain they inflict. Examples of Albee's humor come in several categories:

Wit As an example (there are many)—George responds to Martha when she has changed into a revealing outfit: "Why, Martha . . . your Sunday chapel dress!"

Farce George appears with the shotgun that "explodes" into a colored parasol. Also, George opens the door to their guests as Martha screams "Screw you!"

Insult humor George and Martha are expert at pointed bitchery. Their insults are accurate, deadly, yet often hilarious. (Martha to George: "If you existed I'd divorce you.")

Black humor Albee's ability to evoke laughs out of the darkest of situations is one of his hallmarks. Black humor (an influence of the Theater of the Absurd) is used throughout the play, from the "games" that turn out to be psychological torture to the description of Martha's father as a white mouse who nibbled the warts of his second wife. There are those who feel that the whole notion of the imaginary child is an elaborate "sick joke."

Crude humor   A great many laughs result from Albee's use of "foul" language: "up yours," "screw you," "angel tits," etc. Not only does this language stand in contrast to the educated diction George and Martha occasionally use, but it demonstrates the low level their battles have reached.

Clichés and Jargon   Absurdist writers often reveal the uselessness of language to communicate by creating dialogue that is filled with clichés and empty phrases. Albee's characters use a great many slang terms and clichés, but usually with an awareness of their emptiness. Phrases like "never mix, never worry," "down the hatch," "the little bugger," "quite a guy," "the little woman," and so on, are used ironically, often with a cutting edge.

Repetition and Parallelism   The dialogue of the play has a great rhythmic feel. Listen for the way Albee repeats words or phrases within speeches or dialogue exchanges to create a variety of rhythms. This technique is used frequently throughout the play, but, for example, read the exchange in Act I when Martha first tells George that she has invited guests. Or review the section of Martha's opening monologue in Act III where she talks of crying all the time. Or examine the repetition of "Yes" in the last moments of the play. For parallelism, look at Martha's beautiful speech in Act III that begins, "George who is out somewhere there in the dark . . . "

These techniques are often used so subtly that you might not notice them, but they give the play an extraordinary unity and sense of movement. There are those who feel that Albee has carefully planned every word, even the "Ohs" and "Unh-hunhs."

Finally, be aware of the wide range of language Albee uses. Each character has his or her own style. George usually speaks clearly, often elegantly. Nick is characterized by his off-hand macho cockiness. Honey's speeches tend to trail off or are filled with prudish inanities. Martha is perhaps the most interesting of them all. Her dialogue moves from the swearing, foul-mouthed cries of a fishwife to the melodic sound of a tender, silver-tongued poet when she speaks of her son. The range of language encompassed by this one character alone marks Albee as an abundantly gifted writer.

Allusions George and Martha's education allows Albee to use a great many allusions in their speeches—literary, historic, and religious. References to Shakespeare, Tennessee Williams, the Punic Wars, the Lamb of God, the Catholic mass, and others make the play a rich tapestry of ideas. Notice that Albee rarely, if ever, uses an allusion without making it work for the characters or the theme. Such allusions add complexity to the work and invite several readings in order to fully appreciate the play.

Symbolism Although *Who's Afraid of Virginia Woolf?* is not as heavily symbolic as some of Albee's other plays, it does use extensive symbolism as part of its literary structure. Some readers see the play as an allegory (a work in which the characters symbolize concepts or ideas). For them, George represents the past (specifically, American ideals of the past); Nick, the threatening future (perhaps Communism); Martha, the primitive and pagan instinct; and Honey (the emotionally unstable daughter of a preacher), the failure of religion. Yet there are others who feel that such a reading asks the play to carry more weight than it can bear.

It is widely thought, however, that George and Martha symbolize the American couple on one level and the failure of the American dream on a higher level. The imaginary child may symbolize not only the spiritual sterility of the modern age, but the illusion that man creates in order to survive the horrors of life. Nick and Honey represent the future in this scheme, a future full of self-interest, deception, and more sterility.

Other more minor symbols are used: the fake gun that suggests George's impotence; the bottle whose label Honey peels off that suggests the "peeling away" of the characters' defenses; the story of the boxing match that suggests the power structure of George and Martha's marriage; and so on.

Albee's later plays (such as *Tiny Alice* and *The Lady from Dubuque*) are often criticized for being top-heavy with symbolism, more symbol than play. But in *Who's Afraid of Virginia Woolf?* he never seems to lose sight of the human dilemma that lies at the play's core.

FORM AND STRUCTURE

The three-act structure of *Who's Afraid of Virginia Woolf?* is unusual in an era when most plays are written in two acts. It's not certain what drew Albee to this form; and it may be that the length and intensity of the play demanded that audiences be allowed two respites from the action instead of one. Whatever the reason, the three acts divide the play neatly into three segments, each of which has its own climactic point. (See the accompanying diagram.)

It is also uncommon for a playwright to name his acts, but Albee's choices provide important clues as to what goes on in each of them. Notice that all the acts are named after rituals.

Act I is called "Fun and Games," a name that is an ironic twist on a common phrase for party activity. The games that go on in this act (and the others) are scarcely fun. They are games of psy-

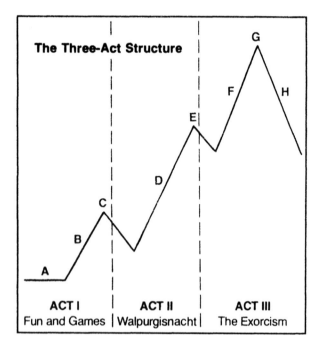

The Three-Act Structure

ACT I	**ACT II**	**ACT III**
Fun and Games	Walpurgisnacht	The Exorcism

chological torment and hostility, with dangerous
repercussions for all concerned. The outcome of
the games is not revealed until the last two acts.

Act II, "Walpurgisnacht," is named after the
evening in German legend when witches gather to
commune in wicked deeds and sexual orgies. It's
in this act that the battle between George and Martha festers to the point of total war, that Nick is
revealed as a ruthless cad, and that the sexual attraction between Nick and Martha grows close to
the point of physical union.

Act III is called "The Exorcism," a title that evokes
the ritual of ridding the body of an evil spirit. This
"evil spirit" is the fantasy of the imaginary child
that possesses George and Martha. George's performance of the exorcism ritual marks a crucial event
of the play, because it probably will alter the couple's life in vital ways.

The Three-Act Structure
Act I
  A. Exposition The characters are introduced, and
     tensions among them are revealed.
  B. Rising Action The tensions increase as Mar-
     tha continues to humiliate George, George acts
     condescendingly toward Nick, and the flirta-
     tion between Martha and Nick continues.
  C. The tension snaps as Martha's verbal assaults
     make George lose his temper, and the accom-
     panying turmoil sends Honey from the room
     to vomit.

Act II
  D. After a short lull in the action as George and
     Nick talk about their wives and jobs, the en-

ergy level increases again as George and Martha continue to square off. Martha punishes George even further by talking about his unpublished novel. He retaliates by attacking her, then proceeds to "get the guests" by exposing their secrets.

E. Climax Goaded by Martha's sexual excursion with Nick, George hatches a plan to "kill" their imaginary son.

Act III

F. After Martha expresses her disappointment with Nick's sexual performance, and Nick's role has turned from male sex symbol to houseboy, George reenters and urges Martha to talk about their son.

G. Falling Action Delivering a shattering blow to Martha, George announces the death of their imaginary son.

H. Denouement or Conclusion Martha and George are left alone to face the future, uncertain of their existence together without their fantasy son.

The Story

Who's Afraid of Virginia Woolf? has three acts, which are not divided into scenes. For the sake of clarity, this guide divides the acts into scenes, based (with some exceptions) on the theatrical device of beginning a new scene whenever a character enters or exits.

ACT I   FUN AND GAMES

ACT I, SCENE I

The setting is the living room of a house on the campus of a small New England college. It is well after midnight. The room is empty, but noises and laughter can be heard outside. Suddenly the door opens, and two people enter the room. Martha, 52, is large and boisterous. Her husband George, 46, is thin with graying hair.

From the very first moments of the play, the differences between Martha and George are marked. She's cranky and belligerent; he tries to pacify her. She's aggressive and loud; he's passive and quiet.

Martha does an imitation of the actress Bette Davis and insists that George identify the movie the quoted line comes from. George tries to put her off: he's tired, it's late, and he's in no mood for guessing games. But it seems that Martha rules the roost. She keeps after him until he reluctantly tries to guess the film.

NOTE: The film with Bette Davis and Joseph Cotten is called *Beyond the Forest* (1949). It probably has no deeper significance to the play than the general parallels between Martha and the bored, restless, ailing character portrayed by Davis. Martha is also bored. Although she's not physically sick, Martha might be considered spiritually sick. And she's certainly discontent, as you'll discover as you read.

The title of Act I is "Fun and Games." Martha's "name that movie" is the first of the games that will be played throughout the night. Be alert for others. Some will be labeled, others will be subtle, but most have serious implications.

George and Martha continue to bicker, and within their bitter exchanges they reveal facts about themselves. George is a teacher at the college, and they have just been to one of the Saturday night parties given regularly by Martha's father, who we learn later is president of the college. Martha chides George for refusing to mix at these parties, and he retorts with a jibe at her loud and vulgar behavior.

These opening exchanges may seem like nothing more than what happens between a "typical" married couple who are tired and have had too much to drink. But you're seeing patterns that are important to the play. Martha tends to bully George, and he accepts her behavior with weary resignation.

Also, the play opens with Martha's "Jesus H. Christ!" This may seem like a casual profanity, but it's the first of many allusions that point to the play's theme of religion.

Now Martha has a surprise for George. She has invited another couple to join them for a drink. Her memory of this couple is blurred, but she does remember that he's "good-looking" and his wife is "mousey."

As you read this exchange about the guests, notice George's reaction. He's not surprised that the male guest is attractive. One of the play's major themes is sex, and sexual jealousy is one aspect of it. Watch George's behavior in this act to note signs that he's jealous of Nick—and that he's not surprised Martha has invited the young couple.

Martha insists she has invited Nick and Honey at the urging of her father, whom she refers to as "Daddy." Why does Martha use this childlike name? Is she trying to be cute, or is there a more serious undertone? Is this a woman who needs to be treated as a child, or who still thinks of herself as a child where her father is concerned? The theme of parent and child figures strongly in the play.

George is put out by Martha's news, accusing her of "springing things" on him. Martha tries to coax George out of his mood by using a childish voice to chant a nursery rhyme: "Georgie-Porgie, put-upon pie!"

NOTE: The second line of the nursery rhyme is "Kissed the girls and made them cry." While this seems an inconsequential taunt, it is an example of Albee's complex patterning. Not only does the nursery rhyme suggest the games indulged in by the characters, but it reminds you that George and Martha often resort to childishness in their relationship. Also, remember this line as you read Act III and hear what Martha has to say about George.

George is unmoved, so Martha tries again to amuse him, singing a jingle that was a hit at the party. It's a parody of "Who's Afraid of the Big Bad Wolf?", a song in the Walt Disney animated-cartoon version of "The Three Little Pigs." The parody substitutes the similar sounding "Virginia Woolf" in place of the animal's name.

NOTE: Virginia Woolf (1882–1941) was a British novelist noted for her experiments in language and fictional technique, such as stream-of-consciousness. (In stream of consciousness a character's thoughts are presented in the often disjointed way they pass through the mind.) Among Woolf's most famous novels are *Mrs. Dalloway, To the Lighthouse,* and *The Waves.* Woolf was at the vanguard of an artistic group in London during the 1920s and 30s that included painters, writers, and philosophers. Since Woolf is considered one of the great literary innovators and influences of the twentieth century, it would not be unusual for her life and work to be discussed at a faculty party such as the one given by Martha's father. Woolf's later years were marked by bouts of insanity, and she drowned herself at the age of 59.

Readers have debated the meaning of the play's title. Some have suggested that Woolf's madness and inclinations to death are meant to be evoked by Martha's character. Others have suggested that it has no deeper meaning than its clever parody— it makes an intriguing title. Albee's only pronouncement about it is his insistence that he used the title because it amused him when he first saw it scrawled as a bit of bathroom graffiti! (The play's working title was "The Exorcism," which became the title of Act III.) Whatever its relevance, you'll hear the jingle used again. Watch for the way its tone changes.

Now the couple argues about whether George found the song amusing. In some ways, this play recalls the classic "battle of the sexes" written about by playwrights for centuries—man and woman striving for the upper hand in a relationship. As you read the play, try to determine in what ways George and Martha are truly battling, seeking to best each other on various issues, and in what ways they are simply arguing out of habit. Perhaps you have a friend with whom you argue constantly, just for the fun of the mental competition. Many people do, and it doesn't always come from mutual dislike. They simply enjoy the give-and-take of matching wits. Others argue because that's the only way they can communicate, and they feel that having a fight is better than not communicating at all. Which of these is true of George and Martha? Or do they all apply in some way? You'll get plenty of evidence to help you make up your mind as the play progresses.

The argument over whether or not George laughed at the song seems insignificant, but it's the first hint of one of the play's major themes: truth and illusion. This will not be the first disagreement about what did or did not happen, about what is real and what is not.

As the argument boils, you can observe the fighting techniques favored by the couple. Martha uses crude insults—"simp," "pig," "you make me puke"—and hits at George's lack of identity—"if you existed I'd divorce you." George takes the role of the submissive intellectual: "That wasn't a very nice thing to say." But don't be fooled by appearances; remember the theme of "truth and illusion."

Notice, too, how quickly the two shift from anger to affection. He calls her "honey" and she asks for a kiss, but soon they're back in the heat of the battle. What do these abrupt changes of tone tell you about George and Martha? Are their antagonisms only on the surface? Or do they simply know each other's vulnerabilities so well that they can pick up the battle in a split second?

Notice George's reaction when Martha asks for a kiss. He evades the issue by giving her a flip excuse, but his avoidance of physical contact may be saying something pertinent about their sex life.

They hammer away at each other, George hitting on Martha's supposed whorish behavior, Martha calling him "a blank, a cipher," as if he were merely an unpleasant figment of her imagination (the theme of truth and illusion again). Does he have no effect on her at all, or does she want him to think he doesn't? Think about this as you read.

The doorbell chimes, and Martha is all set to "party." Still in midbattle, the fight becomes a test of wills as to which one will open the door. Martha wins, but George has a warning for her: she's not to start in on "the bit."

"The bit" that George mentions concerns a child, "the kid." Here is the first reference to a factor central to the play: George and Martha's son. Why doesn't George want him mentioned? What will happen if Martha disobeys George (which she's likely to do)? Suddenly, suspense enters the play. How will the guests change the dynamics of George and Martha's relationship? Will Martha do as she likes and talk about the child?

As George goes to the door, he deliberately goads Martha with insults, angering her to the point where she screams "SCREW YOU!" just as he opens the door. Here Albee has created a wonderful theatrical moment. Imagine how the guests feels as they are welcomed by Martha's "greeting"! Imagine how Martha feels! As for George, there's every indication that he planned the moment. The stage directions tell us that his expression of pleasure comes from Martha's being overheard, not Nick and Honey's arrival.

NOTE: In many plays, the stage directions give only the most basic information. In printed texts of plays, the stage directions are often supplied by a stage manager to indicate how the original production was staged. But in this play, the stage directions are Albee's, and they often give specific clues as to his own intentions about the play. George's expression of glee at the timing of Martha's remark and the arrival of Nick and Honey is a good example of Albee telling us what was on his mind when he wrote the scene.

Don't forget that *Who's Afraid of Virginia Woolf?* is in many ways a comedy. While the implications of the play are very serious, the humor, especially in the first act, almost never lags. The laughter helps the audience to release some of the tensions built up by the emotional demands of the play.

Nick and Honey's arrival gives you one of those releases.

ACT I, SCENE II

The early part of the scene is devoted to the general social discomfort the four feel in this awkward situation. Martha overcompensates for her profanity, George is matter-of-fact, Nick tries to be polite, and Honey can do little more than giggle. You might sympathize with Nick and Honey if you've ever been made uncomfortable by someone you tried to impress.

As the four interact, watch for their behavior patterns, which will intensify as the "party" continues. Nick attempts to comment politely on a painting on the wall, but George tries to put words in his mouth and makes him feel all the more uncomfortable. Why does George immediately put Nick on the defensive? Is he bullying Nick the way Martha bullies him? Or does he suspect that Nick was invited for reasons other than to please Martha's father?

As drinks are poured, George makes it clear that the insults leveled by Martha and him are not likely to abate just because they have guests. He takes a swipe at her drinking habits, and Martha cheerfully replies, "Screw, sweetie." Like all good guests, Nick and Honey try not to notice the verbal brickbats being tossed back and forth.

NOTE: Martha tells George that he has a "Dylan Thomas-y" quality. Thomas was a celebrated 20th-century Welsh poet, equally known for his evoc-

ative verse and for his alcoholism. (He died in 1953
of an alcohol-related disease.) Martha's cynical crack
suggests George's own intellectual power and his
fondness for liquor—a combination that's often
deadly.

When Martha suddenly bursts out with the
"Virginia Woolf" song, the subject turns to that
night's party. Nick and Honey are properly com-
plimentary about Martha's father, who is, after all,
Nick's boss. But it's evident that Martha's father
is a point of bitterness between George and Martha. "There are easier things," says George, than
being son-in-law to the college president. But Martha insists that George simply doesn't appreciate
his advantage, that some men "would give their
right arm" for the chance.

George's reply, that the sacrifice involves a "more
private portion of the anatomy," points to one of
the play's themes—impotence. George's reference
to the loss of his testicles suggests he has been
figuratively castrated by Martha, leading some
readers to feel that Albee is writing about the emotional castration (or domination) of the American
male by the female.

How do you feel about this issue? Is it still pertinent—or is it even more pertinent—in this era's
quest by women for equal rights? The relationship
between male and female has been a hot issue since
Adam and Eve, and a favorite subject for playwrights. Some readers have complained that Albee
reveals intense misogyny (hatred of women) in his
plays. In your estimation, is that a fair criticism of
this play? How does this explosive battling be-

tween the sexes reflect what you've observed about the world? Does a certain amount of conflict exist within every male-female relationship?

When Honey excuses herself, she can't bring herself to use the word *bathroom*. Here is one of the earliest suggestions of Honey's childlike ways and her avoidance of reality.

NOTE: George wryly refers to the bathroom as "the euphemism." A euphemism is a word or phrase that is mild or indirect, used as a substitute for one that is harsh or blunt—such as *passed away* for *died* or *sanitary engineer* for *garbage collector*. George makes fun of Honey's aversion to using the word *bathroom*, but as you will see, her avoidance of reality, suggested by her use of euphemisms, is a major part of her character.

After a few parting words of anger to George, Martha leaves to show Honey the house. As for George, he throws her another warning about mentioning the "you-know-what," the forbidden subject. Martha, of course, refuses to promise anything.

ACT I, SCENE III

Nick and George are alone, and for a time they endure a strained conversation. The conversation bounces among various subjects as the two men talk:

1. THE SCHOOL

You've already seen George's dislike of Martha's father. In this scene you discover his bitterness over his lack of advancement. (He's an associate professor. Most people his age would have achieved the rank of full professor.) The only time he headed the department was during World War II, when most of the male faculty had joined the service.

George's cynicism about the school is revealed in a variety of allusions—the story of the teacher buried in the shrubbery, Martha's father's longevity ("the staying power of one of those Micronesian tortoises"), and a variety of sarcastic names for the college and the town.

NOTE: Although there are tortoises on Micronesia (a group of small islands near the Philippines), those who live for centuries are found in the Galapagos Islands, off the coast of South America. It isn't known whether this slight error is Albee's, or whether he deliberately plants it to suggest that George made a mistake when he attempted to impress Nick. In either case, the image of Martha's father as an ageless tortoise is grim but humorous.

The real name of the town is New Carthage. Albee's choice suggests the ancient empire of Carthage, once a flourishing civilization until it was conquered by the Romans in the Punic Wars (third and second centuries B.C.). Albee seems to be comparing modern civilization with that of the Carthaginians. What are the forces, according to Albee,

that have conquered our civilization? Think about
this question as you read the play.

NOTE: The nicknames George has for New Carthage are drawn from various places. Illyria, an
area of the Balkan Peninsula, is also the idealized
setting of Shakespeare's *Twelfth Night*. *Penguin Island* is a novel by Anatole France (1844–1924) set
on a mythical island destroyed by capitalism. Go-
morrah is the city in the Bible that was destroyed,
along with Sodom, for its wickedness. Parnassus,
George's name for his father-in-law's house, refers
to a mountain sacred to ancient Greek gods.

George also speaks of a disease invented from
the initials of the degrees he holds—Bachelor of
Arts, Master of Arts, and Doctor of Philosophy,
ABMAPHID—which he calls both a "disease of the
frontal lobes" and a "wonder drug."

You'll see that George constantly calls attention
to his disillusionment and disgust with his failure
in the department. Why is he so open about his
flaws? Is he simply honest, or is he punishing himself? George's tendency to dwell on his worst points
suggests a streak of masochism (a tendency to self-
inflict pain or suffering, often for sexual gratification). This is an important characteristic to remember.

2. THEIR PROFESSIONS

George is a historian, Nick a biologist. This is
the first reference to another of the play's themes—
history vs. science. George and Nick are con-

trasted by seemingly irreconcilable philosophies. George is hostile to the notion of a future where everyone is alike. Perhaps you can understand his fear. Where would historians be without the variety of human experience to study? George feels threatened by Nick's profession, although he doubts that anyone learns much from history. Do George's feelings reflect something you've felt about progress and the future of mankind?

NOTE: It's been suggested that Nick's name is meant to evoke that of Nikita Khrushchev, a leader of the Soviet Union from 1953 to 1964. If George's name suggests George Washington and the disintegration of the American revolutionary spirit (as some believe), then this confrontation may represent an East-West standoff, very much in the minds of audiences during the Cold War of the early 1960s. For these readers the play is political allegory as well as psychological warfare.

---

3. THEIR WIVES
George speaks sarcastically about Martha ("Martha is a hundred and eight . . . years *old*") and inquires frankly about Honey. A sly allusion to the frequency of "musical beds" brings to mind the theme of games and gamesmanship while foreshadowing a situation that will occur later in the play.

4. CHILDREN
The subject of children comes up, underscoring another theme: parents and children. Nick and

Honey are childless, but when Nick asks George if they have any children, George's reply is mysterious: "That's for me to know and you to find out." You've already seen George act strangely about their child ("the bit"), but now he's turned it into another game.

Overriding the whole scene are George's attempts to intimidate Nick by acting remote, twisting his words, pulling rank on him. This scene has been compared to a chess game between the two men. How does George keep the upper hand? Remember that Nick *has* to be polite: George is the son-in-law of the college president. But it's still unclear why George toys with his guest, a relative stranger, in such a way.

George calls for Martha, who answers him abrasively, but it's Honey who appears.

ACT I, SCENE IV

Honey returns with two bits of information that infuriate George: Martha is changing her clothes to be more "comfortable," and she has mentioned the forbidden topic—their son—to Honey. George says to himself, "OK, Martha . . . OK," as if he has made a decision based on her behavior. He has warned her about this—now what will he do?

Martha enters, having changed into a dress that makes her look "more voluptuous." George's suspicions that Martha is sexually attracted to Nick have been confirmed—she's on the prowl.

The next several minutes of the play find George increasingly embarrassed. His failure in the history department is contrasted to Nick's early academic success. His "paunchy" body is compared to Nick's athletic achievements. Martha is relentless in her criticism of George, taunting him with the term *swampy*.

Notice how Martha moves from the phrase *bogged down* to the term *swampy*. It's one of many examples of Albee's own verbal agility and the ways he wields it throughout the play.

George does his best to keep his temper from erupting. You may wonder why he allows Martha to treat him this way. Is it the presence of their guests? Is he innately a masochist, who enjoys the suffering? Or is he simply biding his time to deal with Martha in another way? Watch him to see which of these reasons apply.

At the same time, George tries to counter Martha's insults with an elaborate refusal to light her cigarette. It shows again George's tendency to try to use his intellect to demonstrate superiority, but Martha responds with nothing more than a contemptuous "Jesus."

The reference in George's speech to a descent down the evolutionary ladder not only recalls his feeling that he has been dehumanized by Martha, but also connects Martha's behavior with that of a primitive being. Allusions such as this support those theories that suggest Martha represents a pre-Christian, pagan, elemental force in the play. There will be other similar references.

The "body talk" between Martha and Nick reinforces the implied sexual tension between them. Martha is more and more obvious in her comments. At one point in this scene, the stage directions tell you that "there is a rapport of some unformed sort" between them.

You may wonder why Honey seems to notice none of this. The obvious answer is that she's too drunk. Indeed, a great deal of liquor is being consumed by all four! But for all of Honey's inane behavior, there is more to her than meets the eye.

Talk of sports leads Martha to mention a boxing match that occurred during her and George's early marriage. When she ignores his warnings not to tell the story, he angrily leaves the room. But she persists with her tale. At a time when Martha's father was trying to improve the faculty's athletic prowess, he tried to engage George in a boxing match. When George declined, Martha jokingly put on the gloves and surprised George by punching him square in the jaw and knocking him to the ground.

Martha calls the incident of the boxing match both "funny" and "awful," saying, "I think it's colored our whole life." What does she mean? Can such a small event have such an effect? Does she mean that it was symbolic of their relationship, with Martha as aggressor and George as victim? Or does she mean that he's never forgiven her for the humiliation? Perhaps it was the first of the games they've been playing ever since, with serious results. Whatever Martha means, it's this incident, she says, that George uses for not having "gone anywhere" in the history department. Could her father have respect for a man who could be punched out by a woman?

George returns with a "surprise" of his own—a short-barreled shotgun that he aims at the back of Martha's head. As Honey screams and Nick moves to stop him, Martha turns around and George pulls the trigger! But the gun is a toy that shoots a harmless Chinese parasol!

The gun is an important symbol in the play. On one level it is a device to defuse the tension. It allows you to relax a bit as you discover the joke along with the characters.

More importantly, the gun has other meanings. It's yet another game that gives the act its title. Also, it's a metaphorical act of murder that is one of the play's themes. The joke is harmless, but it is prompted out of George's genuine rage, suggesting that he wishes it were real. He kills Martha symbolically for her cruelty—but with a toy gun, suggesting both George's recurring failures and the theme of truth and illusion.

The gun is a sexual symbol, too. Guns are often considered phallic symbols (representing the penis) in literature. George's castration and impotence have already been touched upon in the play; here the theme is given tangible form. Martha emphasizes its sexual overtones when she says to Nick, "You don't need any props, do you, baby?" Martha has again won this round. George has attempted to bring the attention away from Martha's boxing story, but she turns the tables by pointing up George's impotence and Nick's sexual power.

Why then does Martha demand a kiss from George, and then urge him on by putting his hand on her breast? Is she turned on by violence—or by its potential? Or is she transferring her lust for Nick to George? Either way, she is hurt when George turns her down.

NOTE: George wonders if Martha has "blue games" in mind. "Blue" is a term for something off-color or sexual in content. Here the theme of games and gamesmanship appears again, as well as the theme of sex. His accusation will have its echoes later in the play as the action accelerates. Does she have "blue games" on her mind? George's response, "everything in its own good time," foreshadows what's to come regarding these games.

ACT I, SCENE V

Nick leaves the room, and George again brings up the subject of Nick's profession, his work with chromosomes. For the first time Martha learns that Nick is in the biology department, not the math department as she insisted before. When Nick returns, Martha turns this knowledge into a compliment for him—biology puts him "right at the . . . *meat* of things." Martha's sexual allusion continues her open seduction of Nick.

NOTE: When George says that in his mind Martha is buried in cement "right up to [her] neck," it may be a reference to Samuel Beckett's absurdist play, *Happy Days*, in which the main character is buried in a mound of sand, first to her waist, then up to her neck. Such an allusion would reflect Albee's respect for and interest in the absurdists.

George begins elaborating on his earlier conversation with Nick about genetic alteration that will produce "a race of men . . . test-tube bred . . . incubator-born . . . superb and sublime."

NOTE: George's cry "I will not give up Berlin!"
is a reminder of the Cold War struggle for Berlin
that resulted in the wall that divides the city between East and West. This allusion points to the
aspect of the play that underlines the conflict between George (representing American ideals of the
past) and Nick (representing the communistic "wave
of the future").

The reference "one hand on my scrotum" links
George's stand ironically with the earlier allusion
to castration.

Albee gives George the floor in this elegant and
eloquent speech, interrupted only by Nick's mild
protests and Martha's mocking comments. Is
George speaking for Albee's own fear for the future of the human race? It's uncertain, but, obviously, Albee gives George the more persuasive
defense of the two. Nick never tries to deny what
George is saying. Nick even sarcastically agrees,
"And I am the wave of the future."

NOTE: At the time the play was written, the "test-
tube baby" had not been successfully created. The
process, called in vitro fertilization, was carried out
frequently in the 1980s, however. Although genetic tampering was not practiced, there are those
who doubt the morality of fertilizing a human egg
outside the woman's body. Is there a danger in
your mind that George's predictions will come true?

These theories either are lost on Martha or she

chooses to ignore them. Situated very much in the here and now, she's delighted that Nick will be a "personal screwing machine." As for Honey, she stays within her passive naiveté, shocked when Nick uses vulgar language. What must she think of Martha?

Honey changes the subject by asking when George and Martha's son is coming home. Notice the change in George's reaction. Cold fury turns into formal politeness as he repeats the question to Martha. Now Martha is "sorry [she] brought it up."

Remember that George was insistent the child not be mentioned. Now he's changed his tune. Why? Remember his earlier line, "OK, Martha . . . OK." It seemed then that he had resolved to do something to get even. This is the first phase of that plan of action.

NOTE: George refers to his son as "the little bugger." Look for other clichéd terms to describe the boy, terms that suggest the old-fashioned ideal of the All-American child, but that will turn out to have a totally different effect. Later in this scene George will deliberately twist "blond-haired, blue-eyed" into "blond-eyed, blue-haired," hinting that the son might be a different version of this "perfect" child from what one might expect.

Martha is angered by George's prodding. She seeks revenge by telling their guests that George isn't sure the child is his. Even George is shocked by this brazen response, and he insists that his parentage of the child is one of the few things in life he is sure of. This assertion will have ironic implications later in the play.

At one point, Honey corrects Martha's grammar, only to be told that Martha went to college. She also went to a convent when she was young—this despite the fact that she didn't then and doesn't now believe in the existence of God. George insists she's a pagan, one who "paints blue circles around her things."

NOTE: A pagan is a person with primitive religious beliefs that predate formalized religions such as Judaism and Christianity. Women in pagan cultures would often paint their breasts as part of religious or ceremonial rites. George's comment is an insult to Martha and her "primitive" behavior as well as a suggestion that she represents an elemental life force. It serves also as another religious allusion.

In an earlier scene, George spoke of the "evolutionary ladder" and suggested that Martha might be a rung or two below everyone else. Now she is being likened to a pagan and an atheist. Is Martha meant to represent precivilization, a life force that is more instinct than reason? Or does this aspect suggest that she demonstrates a race that God has abandoned because He has been forgotten by them? Readers don't fully agree on the role of religion in this play, but allusions to religious rituals and concepts are so frequent they can't be ignored. Many interpretations are possible, and Albee himself has said he often uses more religious symbolism in his plays than he's aware of. Perhaps the sometimes bewildering array of religious images is meant to suggest spiritual confusion in the modern age. Be aware these allusions exist in the play, and realize that there aren't always easy answers to every ambiguity that Albee presents.

Another interesting exchange occurs when Martha and George disagree over the color of the child's eyes. George tells Martha, "Make up your mind." Watch for clues like this that show Martha's indecision about the child. They're important for what will be revealed in the last act.

The subject of eyes leads to another reference to Martha's father. George insists the old man has "tiny red eyes," like a mouse. But Martha reiterates that George dislikes her father only because of George's own "inadequacies." Sick of hearing the same old song, George leaves to get more liquor.

ACT I, SCENE VI

While he's gone, Martha elaborates on the mutual dislike between her husband and her father. As she tells the story of her early life, Nick and Honey interject polite comments and occasionally bicker, but Martha's in no mood to indulge them. She wants center stage and insists on shutting up her guests if they interrupt.

It's been suggested by some readers that, in a play that depends so heavily on games and rituals, this entire "party" may be a ritual, one that Martha and George perform often for guests. They act out their hostilities and describe themselves and each other to whomever they can talk into visiting them.

The script may change slightly, depending on the audience, but it's basically the same set of arguments and confessional speeches. This one about her father may be one of Martha's mainstays; it helps to explain herself to others. Watch for evidence that might support this theory. Also, look for this party to take a dramatic turn that will differentiate it from all others in the past.

Martha's story contains two thematic threads. Her close relationship with her father ("I absolutely worshipped him") suggests that he is as much of a God to Martha as is anything else in her life. It also reminds you that parent/child relationships are important in the play. You're also told of Martha's early sexuality in the story of her affair with the gardener.

NOTE: Martha's reference to Lady Chatterly comes from D. H. Lawrence's novel *Lady Chatterly's Lover* (1928), banned for obscenity for many years after its publication. It tells the story of a sexual relationship between an upper-class married woman and her gamekeeper.

Martha takes time from her story to continue her blatant seduction of Nick, but he declines to carry it any further—especially with Honey nearby.

Martha indicates that George came along as a possible successor to her father. What does this tell you about her fierce disappointment in George? Did she want him as a father substitute? Has he failed by not being as strong or as successful as her father? The notion of a woman looking for a second father in the man she marries is not new. You'll learn something about Martha's father in the third act that will help you decide if this theory is true.

NOTE: Martha's reference to an "albatross" alludes to the long poem "The Rime of the Ancient Mariner" by Samuel Taylor Coleridge (1772–1834). In the poem an albatross is a symbol of bad luck, and ultimately of death. Martha's allusion may be a subconscious comment on her own self-image as a burden to her father.

George returns in the middle of Martha's story to hear her express surprise that she "actually fell for him." The suggestion here is that Martha and George once loved each other. Are there hints that they still do?

As usual, though, Martha goes too far. Ignoring George's warnings to stop, she continues to talk of her father's expectations for George and the way they were dashed when George turned out not to have the "stuff." Again George warns her, but Martha moves ahead, now "viciously triumphant," and declares him "A great . . . big . . . fat . . . FLOP!"

It's clear that George is humiliated because Martha has made his failures so public. But the pressures on him to succeed have built up over the years and are a constant source of pain for him. Albee seems to be saying that the quest for success often demands a heavy price, particularly if the goals are not reached.

Is it so terrible that George is an associate professor rather than a full professor? Perhaps you have felt burdened, in a lesser way, pressed to achieve a goal that may not seem so important once you've reached it. Whether the pressure comes from someone else or from yourself, you might have felt yourself the victim of an unspoken rule that says you must succeed no matter what the cost. George's constant humiliation under Martha's cruelty is a reminder of the price many pay for striving to reach an elusive reward. Do you think this is a particularly American malady?

Furious, George smashes a liquor bottle to stop Martha, a gesture that may be another symbol of George's impotence. The gesture doesn't work, because Martha merely chides him for wasting good liquor—something he can't afford.

George, near tears, begs her to stop and begins a reprise of the "Who's Afraid of Virginia Woolf?" song. The song is sung now in angry desperation as George hopes to drown out Martha's cruel tirade about his wasted career. It succeeds in stopping Martha only when Honey mindlessly joins in.

The song finally has its effect and Martha screams for the two to "STOP IT!" Is Martha intimidated in some way by the song? Or is she merely frustrated by its innocuous chant? (Remember that this was the woman who laughed heartily at it earlier.) Martha's annoyance with the song foreshadows the song's use later in the play.

Honey rushes from the room, threatening to vomit, and Nick rushes after her. Martha follows them, but not before looking at George contemptuously as she leaves.

George is left alone. The act has built to a peak of dramatic tension, as two of the characters' emotions have undergone enormous strain. There is no indication in the stage directions of how George looks at this moment. If you were directing the play, how would you want George to appear? Defeated and humiliated? Or even more determined to get the better of Martha? Either of these choices is possible, depending on how strongly you feel already that George will end up as the hero of the play. Right now it seems as if Martha has won the first battle. But there is every chance that George may yet win the war—if, indeed, there is to be a victor at all.

ACT II   WALPURGISNACHT

ACT II, SCENE I

A short time has passed since the end of Act I. George is still alone in the room as Nick comes back to tell him that Honey is feeling better. For a few moments, the two engage in a brief ping-pong match of words, each confusing the other's reference to *she*. This comic interchange allows the audience to relax a bit after the tensions of the last act.

A relatively quiet scene follows as the two men talk. The natural hostility between them has not entirely disappeared. Nick admits that he finds George and Martha's behavior embarrassing, and wonders why they air their disagreements so publicly. George furiously calls Nick "smug" and "self-righteous," but he does agree that he and Martha don't make a pretty "spectacle." (The word *spec-*

tacle supports the theory that George and Martha "air their dirty linen" in front of others, since "spectacle" suggests a public display.)

As Nick confesses to being impressed by George and Martha's "skill" at these battles, George says that Nick practices a "pragmatic idealism." (*Pragmatic* means "practical." Idealism is the pursuit of high or noble principles.) In what way does this term apply to Nick?

NOTE: Nick says, "Flagellation isn't my idea of good times." Flagellation is the practice of whipping, used both by certain religious sects for self-discipline and by people engaging in sadomasochistic sex. In what ways do George and Martha engage in metaphoric flagellation? Does the practice extend to Nick and Honey?

A discussion of Honey's sicknesses (she gets sick "regularly") leads to Nick's admission that he married Honey because she was pregnant—or at least he thought she was. Honey had had a hysterical (false) pregnancy. Once they were married, the symptoms disappeared. Remember this fact about Honey because it's related to a number of the play's themes.

A reference to Nick's choice of drink, bourbon, prompts George to tell Nick a story about something that happened when George was 16 and went to a bar during Prohibition with a group of friends. One of these friends was a boy who had "accidentally" shot his mother. This boy innocently ordered "bergin" (meaning bourbon whiskey) at the bar and soon had the entire roomful of people laughing at his mistake. Sometime later, George tells Nick, the boy was driving along a country road, his father beside him. Swerving to avoid a porcupine, the boy hit a tree, and the father was killed. Since then, the boy has been in an asylum and has not uttered one sound.

This speech is one of the most controversial in the entire play. In the stage directions, Albee requests that there be a five-second pause after the speech—a long time on stage—suggesting that Albee feels the speech is very important.

Some readers believe that George is talking about himself, that the story actually happened to him. Others feel that the story is an invention, created to amuse the guests. It's also possible that the story is an allegory that represents the young boy's (George's?) feelings of hatred for his parents. These readers see the asylum as an allegorical representation of George's adult years as a teacher and husband of Martha, trapped and not uttering one sound—that is, having done nothing of significance since then. The "bergin" story will come up later in the play in a way that may help you decide which interpretation makes the most sense.

George makes another puzzling reference to the insane, commenting on how slowly they age, maintaining "a firm-skinned serenity." If George feels he has been in a symbolic asylum for several years, the allusion might be to himself (he has referred earlier to his leanness and firm flesh). Nick's attempts to draw George out on the subject result in George's wistful "Some things are sad, though." His baffling comment is never fully explained.

The talk returns to children and pregnancies.

George mentions that "Martha doesn't have pregnancies at all," which Nick assumes to mean that Martha *no longer* has pregnancies. Considering Albee's precision with language, is Nick correct? Consider this a clue to something that George and Martha have yet to reveal. Another subtle hint is in George's reference to the child as "a bean bag," a child's toy.

NOTE: George's reference to the child as "the apple of our three eyes" is another example of Albee's use of maxims and clichés ("Blond-eyed, blue-haired") in ways that deliberately reverse them. This is a common technique of some absurdists.

He also calls Martha a Cyclops, a gigantic beast in Greek mythology with only one eye in the middle of its forehead.

Martha interrupts briefly, just enough time for her and George to exchange a rapid series of insults in French.

NOTE: The English translations of the words that George and Martha hurl at each other are "monster," "pig," "beast," "scoundrel," and "whore." Their brief "act" shows you not only that they are multilingual fighters, but that they are so practiced in their battles they can engage in showing off for the guests without missing a beat.

Before Martha interrupted, George was about to

"set [Nick] straight" about something Martha had said. After Martha leaves, that issue is dropped. What do you think George wanted to talk about? It's impossible to know, but it might have been about the child. Remember this moment after you've read the play, and decide whether the play might have ended differently had George and Nick not been interrupted.

Nick seems to be on a confessional streak as well. He corroborates George's guess that he married Honey for her money as well as because of her supposed pregnancy. They had known each other since childhood, and the marriage was simply "taken for granted."

NOTE: George speaks of "Chinese women," a reference to a crude joke. Nick's joke about cretins (someone with a congenital mental deficiency) is a pun on the inhabitants of the island of Crete (Cretans).

Both men have something in common. Both have fathers-in-law with money. Honey's father was a semifamous preacher who "spent God's money" and "saved his own." Martha's father inherited money from his second wife, Martha's step-mother.

When Nick says that Martha never mentioned a stepmother, George allows that "maybe it isn't true." Is this another invention of George's, or just an attempt to play with Nick's mind? Either way, the theme of truth and illusion is in evidence again.

That Honey is the daughter of a corrupt preacher has led some readers to feel that Albee is indicting the failure of religion in our lives, that he considers it a collection of corrupt and useless institutions. Certainly Honey, seemingly inane and idiotic, constantly sick or giggling, doesn't suggest that religion has produced healthy offspring. As you've seen, it isn't always easy to understand what Albee has up his sleeve with his religious allusions, but this one is fairly clear-cut. There seems no other reason for Honey to be a preacher's daughter than as an acerbic comment on the state of religion.

The rest of the scene details Nick's "plans" to get ahead at the college. Half-joking and half-serious, he talks of looking for the weak spots, taking over some courses from older teachers, and seducing a few "pertinent" faculty wives.

George pretends to go along with the joke, even to the point of agreeing that Nick had better head right for Martha and "mount her like a goddam dog." After all, she's the daughter of the president. Then the joke stops. George is certain that Nick is serious in these plans.

At this point, which of the two men seem less admirable? George, with his self-pity and passivity? Or Nick with his coldhearted ambition? Perhaps both men seem weak and unworthy of your respect. But is one more humane than the other? Does one seem to care more than the other?

Most readers would give the nod to George. In the next few moments, he tries to advise Nick, warning that he'll be "sucked down" into the "quicksand" of the college if he isn't careful. And George has been there. Despite his dislike of Nick, he offers the younger man a "survival kit." Nick, "the wave of the future," has only contempt for George and his advice.

Here is the first time that George reaches out to

another character, without irony or sarcasm. He tries to "make contact," to "communicate," and all Nick can say is "UP YOURS!"

George's response is another eloquent attempt to define civilization: "communicable sense . . . morality . . . government . . . art." And just when society is brought to the point where there's something to lose, what's the sound that is heard? "Up yours." In short, man has created a civilized society only to see it jeered at by the generation of the future.

This scene has shown you another standoff between history and science, between past and future. Which do you think has the stronger case? Where do you think Albee stands?

NOTE: *Dies Irae* is Latin for "Day of Wrath." The words are from a hymn in Latin concerned with the Day of Judgment. The hymn is sung during requiem masses in the Roman Catholic church. The use of the term foreshadows another, more complex function of the hymn later in the play.

ACT II, SCENE II

Martha returns with Honey, a bit unsteady but back on her feet. Honey alludes to a bout of appendicitis that turned out to be a false alarm. George and Nick exchange glances. They know she's referring to her false pregnancy, but does she know it? Is this a deliberate lie, or just a myth she has come to believe? The line between truth and illusion may be blurred for Honey, too.

Martha launches into another story about their son, and it soon leads to an ugly squabble about which of them was the worse parent. Martha says that George made the child throw up all the time, while George insists that Martha had sexual designs on the child—"fiddling at him all the time." When George admits that he never wants to talk about their son except when he and Martha are alone, he's making an important point.

Martha scores two blows at George by mentioning that he used to drink "bergin" and by referring to a book he once wanted to publish. You'll soon see why these are sore points with him. He declares he has to find a new way to fight Martha, and the imagery of war is blatant: "guerrilla tactics," "internal subversion."

The suggestion that they dance creates a scene that is a perfect metaphor for the characters. Notice how each of them responds to the idea. George first tries to sabotage the suggestion by playing classical music, but then sits at the side and makes cynical comments. For a while, Honey dances by herself, self-absorbed and oblivious to what's around her. Martha and Nick dance closely, with a great deal of sexual innuendo and eroticism. George's sexual comment to Honey ("monkey nipples") appears to mean nothing; he hardly seems interested in her at all.

NOTE: George comments that Martha will "put on some rhythm she understands . . . *Sacre du Printemps,* maybe." He's referring to ballet music (in English, *Rite of Spring*) by Igor Stravinsky evoking an old Russian pagan legend, in which a dance is performed for the fertility of the soil. In the legend, a maiden dances herself to death as a sacrifice. This allusion reminds you of the theme of fertility, of Martha as a pagan creature, and of the sense of ritual inherent in the play. As Martha and Nick dance, George refers to their dance as "a very old ritual . . . old as they come."

For the first time, a note of annoyance is struck between Nick and Honey. "You're always *at* me when I'm having a good time," she says. Little by little it's beginning to be revealed that all is not well with this "perfect" couple.

As if George is not humiliated enough by Martha's openly sexual conduct with Nick, she deepens the wound by telling one of his deepest secrets in a childlike chant. The secret concerns a novel George wrote that mirrors the story he has just told Nick—about the boy who caused the death of his parents. Now Martha declares that the boy in question was George!

Is she telling the truth? Some readers feel she is. Others point out that she blends fact and fantasy so well that it's hard to tell. True or not, though, the story is potent enough to anger George, particularly since one of Martha's points is that George was bullied and degraded by her father, who refused to let George publish the book.

As usual, George's vocal threats to Martha go unnoticed. In fact, they spur her on. He pulls the record from the turntable, but Martha continues to jeer at him.

Suddenly, there is chaos. Honey wildly screams, "VIOLENCE! VIOLENCE!" as George threatens to kill Martha, grabbing her by the throat and strangling her until Nick can pull him off and throw him to the floor.

You've seen that death and murder is one of the play's themes. Here it is made palpable as George truly seems to want to kill his wife. Pushed to the brink, there is nothing for him to do to reach her but to try physical violence. Albee seems to be saying that people resort to violence when all else fails, but that it's no substitute for true communication. Do you agree with Albee's implications? What evidence do you see in the world that suggests he's correct?

Once again Martha is linked with godlessness as George calls her a "satanic bitch."

ACT II, SCENE III

The aftermath of the battle finds George licking his wounds, suffering "a profound humiliation." But if you think he's ready to retreat, you're wrong. He's ready for more games now that they have successfully played "Humiliate the Host."

As George talks of games they have played or could play, the theme of gamesmanship is clearly articulated. "Hump the Hostess," of course, refers to Nick's planned sexual conquest of Martha. Now George suggests a new game, "Get the Guests."

Why does George intend to take out his anger on Nick and Honey? Is he jealous of their apparent success? Is he resentful of Nick's overt sexual approach to Martha? Or does he try to get at them because he can't get at Martha? Whatever he does to her, she bounces back with a devastating rejoinder.

Some have observed that George and Martha are cruel without motivation. Nick and Honey in this context are the chosen victims for the evening, not only as audience members for George and Martha's "show," but as targets for the hosts' excess savagery. Whatever the reason (perhaps a combination of all of these), George is now out to get the guests.

George's technique is to tell of a second novel, which mirrors the courtship and early marriage of Nick and Honey. Notice that George reverts to a slangy, casual style to drive home the story— "Blondie," "upchuck," "champeen"—also mingling academic jargon ("historical inevitability") and biblical rhythms ("Godly money ripped from the golden teeth of the unfaithful").

At first Honey grasps only bits of the story, remarking on its familiarity. But once the impact of what George is saying cuts through her alcoholic haze, she's devastated. Nick has told their secret! She responds typically, by rushing from the room to throw up.

Nick is understandably furious at George, but George suggests that Nick "make the best of things," and "pick up the pieces." Nick responds with a threat to make George regret what he's done, vowing to become the cunning, ambitious cad George has accused him of being. But George insists that Nick already is; he simply doesn't know it.

NOTE: George remarks to Nick: "You gotta have a swine to show you where the truffles are." Truffles are a rare and expensive form of fungus used in gourmet dishes. Swine (pigs) are used to find

the truffles, which grow underground. The
expression suggests that you often have to put up
with a lowly animal (or person) in order to arrive
at the truth. Nick is more concerned with the damage George's story has inflicted on him rather than
with its effect on Honey. It reveals that he's as
crass and self-interested as George has thought.

With another threat, Nick leaves the room to see
to Honey.

ACT II, SCENE IV

Martha and George are alone, and their anger
ripples under the surface. They're like two prize-
fighters pacing, ready for battle.

In the argument that ensues, George and Martha have it out for the first time in the play. The
scene is important, too, because of the consequences it has for the rest of the play.

Martha is disgusted with George. Why? Does
she really care about Nick and Honey, or does she
merely have to be combative, no matter what the
situation? Perhaps this time George has gone too
far, even for Martha.

George can't understand her fury. Isn't she turned
on by "blood, carnage, and all?" Besides, after her
attacks on him, how can she berate anyone for
cruel behavior? He accuses her of making her own
rules, which underscores the sense that this "game"
of hostility is one they play all the time.

The sadomasochistic aspects of their relationship surface as George insists he cannot stand being
torn apart any longer and Martha counters that

she's tired of "whipping" George. Martha's response to his cry cuts close to the bone: "YOU CAN STAND IT! YOU MARRIED ME FOR IT!" George calls Martha's accusation a "desperately sick lie," but you've seen evidence to the contrary. Why else would he put up with Martha's abuse, even calling attention to his own failures? Maybe he's not aware of how much he needs her treatment of him to remind him that he's alive.

The argument grows as each searches for a way to deliver the knockout punch. Martha vows to make him sorry he didn't die in "that automobile" accident. (Again it's not clear if the accident was real.)

According to George, Martha is having trouble distinguishing truth from illusion: she has started playing "variations on [her] own distortions." He suggests he may have to commit her to an asylum.

George's threat pushes her to the breaking point. In a long speech, she describes how their marriage has gone "SNAP!" It's a cry for communication, detailing her attempts to "get through" to him. But those attempts have failed. George agrees that there is no time any more when the two of them could "come together."

This is a powerful scene: The two are raw and bleeding, but still eager to fight. When Martha attacks George's failures and his lack of identity, George counters by calling her "sick" and "a monster" (accusations she fiercely denies). Their knowledge of each other's vulnerabilities is never shown clearer than in this scene. This play is one of the most painful portraits of marriage that has ever been written for the stage, and this scene may be its most devastating. A man and a woman who may once have loved each other, are savagely tearing each other to pieces because hatred is all that's left.

The two declare "total war." The stage directions call for them to "seem relieved . . . elated." Why? Are George and Martha invigorated by these battles? Or do you think they feel something climactic is about to happen now that the battle lines have been drawn for "total war"? It may be that the relief comes from knowing that total war means that one of them will finally be victorious and the years of exhausting fights will come to an end.

ACT II, SCENE V

Nick returns with the news that Honey is lying on the cool tiles of the bathroom floor. Notice that throughout the play Albee has cleverly made it plausible for Nick and Honey to remain at George and Martha's, despite the fact most people would have fled long ago. At crucial moments, Honey gets sick, making it impossible for her to leave. Also, remember that Nick hangs around because Martha is the daughter of the president. In addition, he may have plans to seduce her this very night. Even so, some readers have questioned whether anyone would stay where there is so much hostility and violence in the air.

As George goes for ice, Nick and Martha are left alone. Martha continues her lustful pursuit, now boldly running her hand along Nick's thigh and asking him to kiss her. He resists, alluding to George nearby in the kitchen, but she urges him on. As the two become more involved, George comes in, watches them silently, then smiles and leaves. What does he have up his sleeve?

Nick begins to get carried away, moving a bit too fast even for Martha. George announces his return by singing the "Virginia Woolf" jingle, giving the couple enough time to break up their clinch. He reports that Honey is lying asleep on the bathroom floor, sucking her thumb and curled up in the fetal position. (Here Albee portrays the childlike Honey as a baby, returning to the womb, perhaps to avoid reality.)

NOTE: The allusion to "the worm turns" is taken from Shakespeare, *Henry VI, Part Two:* "The smallest worm will turn, being trodden on." The line suggests that even the lowliest creature will survive persecution and seek revenge on its tormentor. How does this apply to George? Martha's claim that his path leads nowhere but to the grave is a reminder of the theme of death.

George and Martha continue their destructive competition. He announces he's going to sit quietly and read. The implication seems to be that he's out to infuriate her by pretending not to notice her open flirtation with Nick. And he succeeds. Since Martha would rather be fought with than ignored, she goads George by announcing that she's "necking with one of the guests." His reply (revealing Albee's humor) succeeds in escalating her wrath: "Oh, that's nice. Which one?"

Twice in this scene Martha brushes up against the door chimes. Some readers feel that the chimes represent those rung during certain important moments of a Catholic mass.

Finally, George turns on Martha "with great loathing" and almost dares her to take Nick to bed. Nick goes to the kitchen at Martha's request, and she confronts George: Get off this "kick," this haughty indifferent attitude, or she will go to bed with Nick. George pretends that he couldn't care less, and Martha follows Nick, threatening to make George sorry he made her want to marry him.

Alone, George reads aloud. The passage is from *The Decline of the West* by Oswald Spengler (1880–1936), a German philosopher. The influential book, published in the 1920s, contended that most civilizations pass through just one life cycle and that Western civilization had entered its period of decline. The chosen passage could echo his own marital situation: "crippling alliances," and "a morality too rigid to accommodate [him]self." In your opinion, is the morality implied by the play "too rigid"—or not rigid enough?

Suddenly George gives vent to the tension that has been building up throughout the scene as he has watched his wife blatantly pursue another man. Uttering a sound that's "part growl, part howl," he flings the book at the chimes, and they ring for the third time.

Now George shows his true anguish. He's clearly hurt by Martha's behavior but can't let her know it. For her part, Martha probably doesn't want to go to bed with Nick—why else would she announce her plans over and over to George? But this is a game to them. Neither will give the other satisfaction by admitting defeat. If only once one of them would move to stop what neither of them wants, the game might be over and they might reach some understanding. But neither does. You've probably observed this kind of behavior in certain adults; children frequently act in this way. As you have seen, George and Martha often behave like overgrown children, but the consequences of their games are deadly serious.

ACT II, SCENE VI

Honey wanders in. The chimes have awakened her. Still half asleep, she rambles on about a dream of being naked, cold, and frightened, with "someone there." Then she blurts out, "I . . . don't . . . want . . . any . . . children. I'm afraid!" George immediately comprehends that Honey has been secretly using contraceptive devices because she can't admit to Nick that she fears childbirth.

Some readers feel George guesses Honey's secret too quickly and too conveniently. Others say his intuitive guess is plausible since Nick earlier spoke of Honey's frequent bouts of illness, to which George responded, "You can tell time by her, hunh?" George's question probaby alluded to Honey's cycle of fertility. Does he leap to the correct conclusion because he's a keen judge of character (better even at guessing this than Nick, who is interested only in himself?) or because it's necessary to the play? There may be an element of truth in each opinion.

Honey doesn't realize that George knows her secret. As she continues, she reveals herself in two poignant lines. "I want . . . something" suggests that nameless void that many people endure—wanting something but not knowing what it is or

how to achieve it. "I don't want to know anything!" reveals her need to close herself from the
truth, from reality, something you have seen her
do throughout the play. What ways do the other
characters have of shutting out reality?

George tries to make Honey aware of what's
going on in the kitchen, which he calls "a dry run
for the wave of the future." What is he suggesting?
That the future holds nothing but a mindless sexual union? That the biologist and the pagan are
joining to create a new race?

George indicates that those unhappy with the
present can either contemplate the past (as he has
done) or alter the future. "And when you want to
change something . . . YOU BANG! BANG! BANG!
BANG!" On one level these "bangs" suggest a slang
term for sexual intercourse. But they may also represent the destruction of the world, a nuclear holo-
caust. For George, Nick and Martha's selfishness
and lust may be indicative of the breakdown of
morality that will eventually destroy the world. Do
you agree that Albee's expression of fear for the
human race seems more relevant today? Is it better
to "contemplate the past" or to "alter the future?"

George takes out his fury on Honey ("you sim-
pering bitch"). But as she keeps asking who rang
the doorbell, he concocts an ingenious plan to have
the final revenge on Martha. He informs Honey
that a message has arrived telling him their son is
dead. Oblivious to Honey's pained reaction ("I'm
going to be sick"), he quietly rehearses how he will
tell Martha the news. As the act ends, he stands,
laughing and crying at the same time.

What is George up to? Is he playing a cruel joke
on Martha? If so, why is his laughter mixed with

tears? Since the son has been such a mysterious element in the play, you may be even more puzzled now. Perhaps you already suspect the truth. Either way, Albee has created an intriguing ending to the act. Knowing the importance of the child to Martha, you must wonder what kind of impact George's news will have on her.

Act II is called "Walpurgisnacht" (or Walpurgis Night), from a German legend about witches who meet on the last day of April. The rendezvous includes rituals of evil and wild sexual orgies. Having read this act, why do you think Albee chose to name it after this event? Are these characters symbols of evil, gathered to do harm? Or is only one of the characters evil? If so, which one? Is it Martha (whom George has referred to as a "devil" and a "satanic bitch")? Is it Nick, whom some feel was named for "Old Nick," an archaic term for the devil? Is his and Martha's sexual union meant to suggest the orgy practiced by the witches?

Any or all of these interpretations might be true, but remember not to look for simplistic patterns. George might recall St. George, the English saint who conquered evil as represented in the form of a dragon, but the play is too complicated and includes too many ambiguities, to be considered a simple matter of good vs. evil. As you will see, George's actions in the third act don't provide an easy answer to the characters' problems. The days when good and evil seemed clear-cut concepts are over. Albee seems to be describing a situation and pointing to human problems in the modern age, rather than prescribing remedies.

Another possibility is that the title "Walpurgisnacht" might have been used by Albee to evoke the sense of evil, mystery, and lust that pervades the play, rather than having a specific application to the plot.

ACT III   THE EXORCISM

ACT III, SCENE I

You have seen an exhausting series of encounters between George and Martha. Scarred and bleeding, they were still on the attack as the second act ended. She seemed to be on the verge of going to bed with Nick, and George had decided to tell her that their beloved son is dead. His decision marked the play's climax, the point where the play reaches the highest point of tension. What will happen now? How will this difficulty be resolved? Which of the two will win this monumental battle, and what effect will it have on them? And what will happen to Nick and Honey as a result of their exposure to the ferocity of George and Martha?

Martha is alone as the act begins. Drunk and exhausted, she talks to herself in a rambling speech that gives you the first real glimpse of Martha. It is a frightening look at a woman full of desperation and self-pity.

Calling for George, Martha expresses her loneliness. She's been "abandon-ed," "left out in the cold." She creates a fictitious dialogue between herself and George, in which they are both penitent and polite. Is this the way they once behaved? Or is this a George and Martha she once hoped they could be? Either way, you see a Martha who, underneath the coarse exterior, is starved for affection.

What has happened between Martha and Nick?

The only clue you're given is when Martha says, "Hump the Hostess! Fat chance."

The fact that she's alone, without an audience, probably allows you to believe her more fully than at any earlier point of the play. Here she admits what she has vehemently denied before—that her father does have red eyes—red, she says, because he cries all the time.

You've now heard several of Martha's views of her father. In the beginning of the play she defends him vehemently against George's criticisms, then says she "worships" him. Now she admits he "cries all the time," perhaps reflecting his disappointment in Martha and George. Some readers suggest that Martha suffers from an unfulfilled Electra complex, a psychological affliction named for the character in Greek tragedy who helped her brother kill their mother out of love for her father. Perhaps one of Martha's major problems is her wish to find a father substitute, and her intense disappointment that George (nor any other man) can replace the object of her unrequited love.

She admits that she and George cry all the time, too, and describes how their tears are turned into ice cubes to replenish their drinks. Martha's metaphor painfully evokes the cycle of their lives—the anguish that's numbed by alcohol, with frozen tears to cool their drinks.

Searching for a phrase to describe the futility of it all, she tries to remember "up the spout" and "down the drain" but ends up confusing them.

NOTE: A sudden reference to "THE POKER NIGHT" comes from a scene in Tennessee Wil-

liams's *A Streetcar Named Desire*, in which the animal force of one character is first seen to threaten
the spiritual fragility of another. Some of that play's
themes—sexuality, violence, the extinguishing of
the human spirit—are similar to those of *Who's Afraid
of Virginia Woolf?* You'll see another allusion to *A
Streetcar Named Desire* in this act.

By the end of her speech, Martha is reduced to
imitating the sound of her ice cubes—CLINK!—
which, don't forget, are made from her tears.

ACT III, SCENE II

Nick comes in, bewildered by everyone's behavior: Honey is back on the bathroom floor, Martha
is making strange noises, and George has vanished. Martha assures him that they're all simply
retreating from reality, and that he's no better than
they are.

Then Martha takes a swipe at Nick that confirms
what has been hinted at: Nick was a "flop" in bed.
Nick is defensive but doesn't deny Martha's accusation.

Already in this act you've seen two of the characters revealing that they're not what they seem.
Martha's revelation of vulnerability is in strong
contrast to her earlier aggressive behavior. Now
Nick, "the personal screwing machine," has failed
in that function at a crucial moment. The examples
of "truth and illusion" continue to mount.

Notice the difference in Martha and Nick's relationship! He is angry at her for her appraisal of
his sexual performance, and she responds with a

searing indictment of herself and of all the "gorgeous lunk-heads" like him she has known. Her reference to herself as "Earth Mother" is a reminder of her symbolic role as a primitive life force, but now it has ironic overtones. The Earth Mother engages in a series of "pointless infidelities" that result in nothing. Once again the theme of impotence looms large in the play.

Martha calls these men "poor babies." Does she go after them as child substitutes? If so, what does it say that they are all disappointments? Albee points here to a symbolic sterility that will take on added meaning by the end of the play.

She also has some surprising news for Nick. Of all the men in her life, George is the only one who has been able to satisfy her. Martha responds to Nick's disbelief by asking, "You always deal in appearances?" Here the theme is stated in a question that implies that appearance and reality are often two different things.

In a moving speech, Martha explains the contradiction between how George treats her and how she responds to him. It supports what you may have suspected all along in the play—that so much hate can only come from a great deal of love. Psychological violence is one of the ways these characters have found to let the other know how much they need each other. That people behave this way at all, Albee seems to be saying, is one of life's sad truisms. Do you agree with Albee? Is hate often a mask for undeclared love? Why?

Some of Albee's most effective writing appears in this scene. Notice the rhythms he creates by the repetition of the construction "who" (followed by a verb) and "whom I." It stands in vivid contrast to Martha's usual language.

The speech also reveals Martha's awareness of the games she and George play, when she says that George "keeps learning the games . . . as quickly as I can change the rules." And she poignantly sums up the pain of her life in two other lines: "I do not wish to be happy, and yes I do wish to be happy," and, referring to George, "who has made . . . the mistake of loving me and must be punished for it."

Look again at this last line. Why must Martha punish those who love her? Perhaps the reason is that she doesn't know how to accept love. Or perhaps she thinks so little of herself that she despises anyone who loves someone as unworthy as she. Whatever the reason, she sums up her plight with heartbreaking economy: "George and Martha: sad, sad, sad."

Nick, however is unmoved. In reference to her comment about breaking George's back, he says it had been broken long ago.

NOTE: Martha calls Nick a "gelding" (a castrated horse). This is quite different from her early lustful reaction to him! It also suggests the theme of castration first evoked by George in Act I. Has Martha "castrated" Nick, too? Her reference to herself as a "Gatling gun," an early machine gun, certainly suggests a powerful destructive force.

In the midst of this ugly exchange (which may remind you of Martha's verbal battles with George), the doorbell rings. Martha commands Nick to answer, just as she ordered George to answer the door in Act I. She treats Nick with the same kind

of scorn she usually reserves for George, jeering at Nick's impotence ("Can't you get the latch up, either?").

The doorbell continues to ring, as Martha casts Nick in the role of houseboy. It's the one he has to play if he wants to climb the ladder of success. Now that he's stuck his nose in it, she tells him, he's in it for a while.

Protesting about the pointlessness of Martha's game, Nick goes to the door, while a delighted Martha sings a line from an old song, "Just a Gigolo."

NOTE: Gigolo is a term for a younger man who woos an older woman for financial gain. The song Martha sings was popular in the 1930s. One of its lines is, "Just a gigolo, everywhere I go, people know the part I'm playing." Can Nick be considered a gigolo?

Why doesn't Nick refuse to play the role of houseboy? Does he realize that it's better to go along with Martha's games than to fight her, so long as Honey is still spaced out in the bathroom? Or does this prove how ambitious he really is, willing to degrade himself to please the president's daughter? Your reaction depends on how desperate you think Nick is to get ahead.

ACT III, SCENE III

Nick opens the door for George, whose arms are filled with snapdragons. Speaking in the voice of an old woman, George says, *"Flores para los muertos."*

NOTE: George's line in Spanish is another allusion to Tennessee Williams's play *A Streetcar Named Desire*. It is spoken by an old woman selling "flowers for the dead" outside the window of Blanche duBois, the play's central character. The chant heralds death for Blanche—not physical death, but the death of the spirit.

Remember that George is planning to announce the death of their son. George's arrival with the snapdragons, spouting lines from a play and then pretending he has mistaken Nick for the son, is strange behavior indeed. But perhaps you've already suspected that George's plans and actions are likely to be unorthodox.

Notice, too, the immediate rapport that develops between Martha and George—this time, against Nick. Nick is introduced as the houseboy, and George and Martha respond to Nick's protests by harmonizing: "I'm nobody's houseboy now."

NOTE: Their song is a quickly improvised version of an old song, "I'm Nobody's Baby." Earlier, Martha had greeted George's gift of flowers with the line, "Pansies! Rosemary! Violence! My wedding bouquet!" Not only does her comment include a pun—"violence" for "violets"—but the line may remind you of a scene in *Hamlet*, when the mad Ophelia enters in her never-to-be-used wedding gown, strewing these flowers before her.

When he complains that George and Martha are

"vicious," Nick is greeted by derision. If Nick is about to complain of "vicious children" playing "oh-so-sad games," George says, he can just "screw, baby."

But the collusion between George and Martha doesn't last. His claim that he picked the flowers in the moonlight leads to an argument over whether there is a moon that night. George even insists that the moon disappeared and then returned. A shift of power has occurred. George is now in subtle control, to the point of altering reality.

Other references to "truth and illusion" abound. Nick says, "I don't know when you people are lying," and George responds, "You're not supposed to." And an allusion to George's parents causes Nick to ask, "Was this after you killed them?" "Maybe," says George. "Yeah; maybe not, too," says Martha. George makes the matter explicit: "Truth and illusion. Who knows the difference, eh, toots?"

As Martha and George continue to wrangle about whether he ever went to Majorca, you get a glimpse of the kind of game that brought them to the point of confusion they're at now. George tells a story, Martha disbelieves it, George elaborates on it, and Martha tries to trip him up.

The game does not always please both of them. Martha quietly admits that Nick is not a houseboy, which she seems to say for Nick's benefit, since he thanks her "tenderly." She then says to George, half-pleading, half-hoping, "Truth and illusion, George; you don't know the difference." He replies, "No; but we must carry on as though we did." Her "Amen" suggests both agreement and a religious ritual. Watch them during the rest of

the play to see if they truly know the difference between truth and illusion.

George begins to grow hostile, tossing snap-dragons in a weird parody of Martha's earlier claim that their marriage has gone SNAP! Martha begins to be a bit afraid. Does she sense his behavior threatens something she won't like?

George announces another game, "Bringing Up Baby," and obnoxiously insists that Honey be there too, calling for her like a sow. As Nick goes to get his wife, George soothes a fearful Martha, assuring her that this game will be "real fun"—and the last one they will play before going to bed.

Martha's attempts to touch George tenderly are met with a snarling "Don't you touch me!" Then he grabs her by the hair, commanding her to be alert for what's to come. The "slave" of the early part of the evening has become the "master": George is now in full control. He gives as good as he's received from Martha.

NOTE: George threatens to make Martha's ear-lier game seem "like an Easter pageant," another religious allusion. Easter Sunday is the Christian holiday that celebrates the resurrection of Christ after He was crucified. The play takes place early on a Sunday morning but George is planning a death, not a resurrection.

George finally succeeds in making Martha an-gry. This game will be played to the death, he says; she insists the death will be his. His reply, "You'd be surprised," should be a warning to her about what's to happen.

ACT III, SCENE IV

Nick and Honey come in. She's still very drunk, pretending she's a rabbit and pointedly assuring George that their secret (the death of George and Martha's son) is safe with her.

George takes the floor to summarize the games they've played. Honey has a new one to add: peel the label. George insists that everyone peels labels, and they're about to do it all the way to the marrow. In what way have these four been peeling labels all night?

George moves skillfully to the subject of their son. Ignoring Martha's protests not to talk about him, George describes the boy, reiterating his claim that Martha would climb all over the boy and corrupt him with her wayward habits. His accusations provoke Martha into telling her version of the story, her "recitation."

A recitation suggests something memorized. It is George's word (as well as part of the stage directions), and he prompts Martha in the early part of her story. What does this imply about the child? If you add up the clues that have been planted throughout the play, you may be close to guessing, if you haven't already.

Martha's description of the child is exquisite, perhaps the most beautifully written passages in the play. The details she chooses, from the transparent floating goldfish to the banana boat, evoke a golden, idealized childhood. Could this be the Martha that greeted her guests with a profanity?

As Martha reminisces, George begins to recite Latin prayers from the Catholic requiem mass, the mass for the dead.

NOTE: In addition to the strong religious symbolism of George's prayer, Christ is also evoked when Martha calls the child "poor lamb." This is a common phrase to describe an unhappy or unfortunate child, but it might also be meant to suggest "the Lamb of God," which in Catholic liturgy is another name for Jesus.

This scene also contains the only real change we see in Honey in the play. Martha's heartrending descriptions affect Honey to the point where she cries out, "I want a child." Whether this is a permanent change for Honey is never disclosed.

Martha's story undergoes a change of tone. The child's perfection, she says, was undermined by George's weaknesses: George dragged the son down with him.

Now the two go at each other with their familiar savagery, each accusing the other of failing the son—Martha with her drunkenness and lust, George with his weak will and passivity. Each jealously guards his or her hold on the boy: they both insist they have letters from him that the other hasn't seen.

In an impassioned speech, Martha calls her attempts to protect their son as the one light in the "sewer" of their marriage. Simultaneously, George recites another passage from the requiem mass that begins, "Deliver me, Lord, from eternal death, on the dread day of judgment."

This act is entitled "The Exorcism," which is the ritual involved in casting out demons or evil spirits that have possessed a person's soul. George's quotes from the mass suggest such a ritual.

Honey implores George and Martha to stop what they're doing. Remember that she believes a telegram has arrived announcing the son's death.

George prepares Martha for the news, slowly and deliberately. When he finally tells her their son is dead, the circumstances he describes are precisely those of the boy in the "bergin" story. Some readers feel that this is evidence that the story George has told Nick is pure invention.

Little by little, Nick begins to put the pieces of the puzzle together. When Martha screams, "YOU CAN'T DECIDE THESE THINGS!" he at first attributes her reaction to shock over the news. But when George replies, "YOU KNOW THE RULES, MARTHA!" and "I can kill him, Martha, if I want to," Nick finally comprehends what you may have already suspected—that George and Martha's son is imaginary, yet another of their games, complete with its own set of rules.

NOTE: Some readers who see this play as a religious allegory point to the requiem mass, the three door chimes, the Sunday morning time frame, the "Lamb of God," even the reference to eating the telegram (as a form of communion) as evidence. They feel that the "perfect" child represents Jesus Christ, killed by George in order to save mankind—as represented by George and Martha.

Martha pathetically defends herself. She has clearly stepped over the invisible boundary the two had set: the child is not to be mentioned to anyone else. But Martha's need for the child to be real had overwhelmed her realization that it must be a private matter.

In Latin, George intones "Rest in peace," and then "Grant them eternal rest, Lord," to which Honey (in an uncharacteristic moment of lucidity) gives the proper response, "And let perpetual light shine upon them."

George confirms Nick's suspicion when, in answer to Nick's question, "You couldn't have . . . any?" he responds, "*We* couldn't." For once George shares with Martha the responsibility of their failure to have children.

This revelation is the most crucial of the play. What do you think caused Martha and George to "create" the child? Did the fantasy begin years ago, when the possibility of children was still real? Or did they begin to hope for a child—part of the American dream—as a means of cementing their crumbling relationship? Perhaps the fantasy began as one of their many games: What if we had a child? What would he be like? What would we do with him? Gradually, however, the fantasy began to seem real to them, so real that the idealism of the boy competed with their own bitterness toward each other. They transferred their own hatred and disappointment to the child, accusing each other of destroying their perfect creation. Because it helped them avoid the pain of their lives, George and Martha clung to the fantasy as vital to their survival.

What then does the child represent in the scheme of the play? Some have objected to the imagined son, calling it a theatrical device that Albee pulls out of the hat at the last minute, one that can't be believed. Others defend the choice as an effective symbol of the way many people shut out reality in order to make life bearable. Modern life demands that we create these illusions if we are to avoid madness, Albee seems to be saying. His choice isn't meant to be wholly realistic; it's a technique borrowed from the Absurdists to make his point. Besides, these readers say, the notion of an imaginary son isn't that incredible. Everyone fantasizes about something. George and Martha, in their loneliness and pain, have simply let one fantasy overwhelm them.

Does the imaginary child seem a credible device to you? Is it too far removed from your own experience, or can you understand someone who so fervently wishes for something that it first becomes almost real and then becomes a necessary part of life? Dreams can begin to take on lives of their own. George and Martha's dream apparently has become more real than most.

Why then does George choose to "kill" the child? Simply because Martha broke the rules? There are hints she has done so before ("Just don't start on the bit," he says in Act I, Scene 1). Later in Act III he says, "It was . . . time," as if he saw that they were becoming too dependent on the fantasy, that they were on the verge of spoiling it forever by their jealous bickering.

Another theory suggests that George commits the ultimate act of revenge, striking his blow to win the war at last. Knowing how much Martha needed this fantasy, he destroyed the one thing truly precious to her.

Your own interpretation depends on whether you
see George as a hero or a villain. Remember that
he is killing his own fantasy, too, one that he invented and nurtured in tandem with Martha. Is he
both a sadist and a masochist? You've seen evidence to suggest he is. Or is he truly bringing Martha salvation by freeing her (exorcising her demon)
from this destructive illusion?

George quietly suggests that Nick and Honey go
home. Nick's unfinished sentence, "I'd like to . . ."
suggests he has something to say or something to
offer, but the thought remains incomplete. What
do you think is on Nick's mind? Have he and Honey
been changed in any way by this evening? Their
future is one of the play's many ambiguities.

ACT III, SCENE V

The last moments of the play are in vivid contrast to the first scene. The sharp, obscene language has been replaced by short phrases and
monosyllables. The drunken energy has turned to
exhausted quiet. The sharp-tongued George of
earlier scenes is now gentle, tender. The abrasive
Martha seems frail and complains of being cold.

The dialogue is filled with uncertainty. George
assures Martha that things will be better, but Martha isn't sure, and George adds, "Maybe."

At one point Martha says, "I don't suppose,
maybe, we could. . . ." What is she suggesting?
Going back to the illusion? Beginning a new one?
George merely says no.

The "Who's Afraid of Virginia Woolf?" song now
becomes a lullaby that George sings to soothe Mar-

tha, who answers, "I . . . am . . . George. . . . I . . . am."

Albee has said that the song really means, "Who is afraid to live life without illusions?" Martha's admission that she is afraid reveals her as frail and vulnerable, fearing life without the fantasy that has helped her live. The song she once characterized as "a scream" has become a haunting hymn to her realization that her future is uncertain and full of nameless threats.

What changes has this evening brought to George and Martha's life? Opinions generally fall into three categories:

1. Those who see the play as hopeful feel that the exorcism will lead to more honest communication and clarity in their lives. Now that they have rid themselves of a destructive fantasy, they can progress to rid themselves of their other defenses—liquor, adulterous sex, cruelty—and move closer together.

2. Others see the play as bleak, viewing George and Martha as now totally defenseless against the horrors of the world, like two turtles without their shells. These readers feel that some shields against life's dangers are necessary, and that George's and Martha's child fantasy hurt no one.

3. Still others view the play as simply descriptive, suggesting that this is not a crucial evening for George and Martha, but part of a cycle they are doomed to repeat forever. Many absurdists (such as Beckett) use the technique of the cyclical chain of events to suggest that man can change nothing and learns nothing from his behavior. Readers who

champion this theory feel that George and Martha are engaging in yet another ritual that will repeat itself endlessly, without hope.

These possibilities all exist within the play. Albee has said that he avoids writing plays with easy answers, preferring to challenge and stimulate his audiences. *Who's Afraid of Virginia Woolf?* has no easy answers.

You may not like or admire George and Martha, nor even sympathize with them, but it's likely you recognize the universe they inhabit, because it's one we all share. They attempt to survive in their own way, just as you attempt to survive in yours.

A STEP BEYOND

Tests and Answers
TESTS

Test 1

1. Martha's father _____
   A. is adored by George and Martha
   B. appears in the last moments of the play
   C. is a great influence on Martha's life

2. Martha is upset with George at the beginning of the play because he _____
   A. got drunk and made a fool of himself
   B. made a pass at Honey
   C. didn't participate in the fun

3. Which of these symbols represents sexual impotence in the play? _____
   A. the toy gun   B. the door chimes
   C. the telegram

4. The story of the boy who caused his parents' death _____
   A. is about Honey
   B. might have been invented by George
   C. is told by Martha

5. Which of these words might be applied to Nick? _____
   I. ambitious

II. shallow

III. honest

A. I and II only   B. II and III only

C. all three

6. Nick married Honey   ____

A. a week before the play begins

B. over the objections of his parents

C. because he thought she was pregnant

7. Which of these themes is *not* important in   ____
the play?

A. truth and illusion

B. gamesmanship   C. friendship

8. George and Martha's son   ____

A. died years before the play begins

B. is a figment of their imagination

C. had been committed to an asylum

9. The line "I want a child" is spoken by   ____

A. Nick   B. Martha   C. Honey

10. The title of Act III, "The Exorcism," applies   ____
to

A. Martha's affair with Nick

B. George's announcement to Martha
that their son is dead

C. Honey's inclination to illness

11. Discuss the use of religious symbolism in *Who's Afraid
of Virginia Woolf?*

12. Compare the characters of George and Nick.

13. Discuss the significance of the titles of the three acts:
"Fun and Games," "Walpurgisnacht," and "The
Exorcism."

14. Discuss the use of games in the play.

15. Is *Who's Afraid of Virginia Woolf?* a hopeful play? Defend your answer.

Test 2

1. Honey's father   _____
   A. was a preacher
   B. advised her to marry Nick
   C. represents the devil in the play

2. When Martha tells the story of the boxing   _____
   match, George
     I. laughs heartily
    II. is humiliated
   III. retaliates by bringing out the fake
       shotgun
   A. I and III only   B. I and II only
   C. II and III only

3. George warns Martha about bringing up   _____
   the subject of their son because
   A. he wants to do it
   B. Martha exaggerates their son's
      achievements
   C. the son is a private fantasy

4. The theme of history vs. science is best   _____
   represented by
   A. George's and Nick's professions
   B. Honey's father and Martha's father
   C. the "bergin" story

5. George's speech about "peeling labels" is   _____
   prompted by
   A. Martha's announcement that they're
      out of liquor

    B. Honey, who's lying on the bathroom
       floor

    C. Nick's admission that he had to marry
       Honey

6. Honey's tendency to become ill represents   _____
    A. her inability to face reality
    B. Nick's ambitious drive to the top
    C. George and Martha's treatment of her

7. When Martha says, "SNAP! It went snap!"   _____
   she's referring to
    A. their marriage
    B. her mental condition
    C. George's career

8. George decides to tell Martha their son is   _____
   dead when
    A. Honey wonders why the chimes rang
    B. Martha tells Nick and Honey about
       George's novel
    C. Martha sings "Who's Afraid of
       Virginia Woolf?" at the beginning of
       the play

9. George's novel is about   _____
    A. his marriage to Martha
    B. a boy who caused the death of both
       his parents
    C. his father-in-law

10. The theme of truth and illusion is best   _____
    represented by
    A. the ringing of the door chimes
    B. George and Martha's son
    C. Nick's decision to go to bed with
       Martha

11. Discuss the function of Nick and Honey in *Who's Afraid of Virginia Woolf?*

12. Discuss the uses of the song "Who's Afraid of Virginia Woolf?"

13. What is the importance of children and babies in the play?

14. What is the importance of the imaginary child in *Who's Afraid of Virginia Woolf?*

15. In what ways do Nick and Honey change during the play?

ANSWERS

Test 1

1. C	2. C	3. A	4. B	5. A	6. C
7. C	8. B	9. C	10. B		

11. Religious allusions and symbols appear throughout the play, but readers don't agree whether the symbols are meant to suggest the hope of religion or its failure. References to Christ and God are frequent (often expressed as curses or hidden in common expressions). There are also religious symbols (both Christian and pre-Christian)—for example, in Martha's role as "earth mother," in the satanic rites of Walpurgisnacht, and in the ritual of exorcism that accompanies George's attempts to rid Martha of the "possession" that haunts her (their imaginary child). George reads a passage from the Catholic mass for the dead as Martha describes their son to Nick and Honey. Other more subtle hints include the ringing of the door chimes three times (to suggest the beginning of a mass), George's claim to have eaten the telegram (communion), and Honey's father, a corrupt preacher. Readers disagree over the meaning of

many of these symbols, but few deny that they make up a great deal of the fabric of the play.

12. Because of the differences in their ages, George and Nick represent two different generations. George is generally passive, weakened by his lack of success and by Martha's constant humiliation of him. Nick is young, ambitious, amoral, eager to get ahead by whatever means it takes. The two are also contrasted by their professions. A historian, George is also representative of a humanist, one who is interested in human values—in his case, with a particular interest in the past. A biologist, Nick represents both the future and the clinical, coldhearted approach to life that threatens to rob mankind of its individuality. Albee ironically turns the tables on the characters when George is shown to be the one in control and the only one who has ever satisfied Martha. Nick, "the stud," is impotent in his sexual encounter with Martha and becomes the "houseboy," the subservient one.

13. "Fun and Games" is an ironic use of the phrase often associated with parties. It suggests not only the psychological games that George and Martha play with each other as a substitute for communication but also the "games" played with Nick and Honey. They become unwitting victims of George and Martha's need to include others in their web of mental cruelty.

"Walpurgisnacht" means, literally, "Night of the Witches." In European folklore, it is a night when witches meet to indulge in orgies. It is in this act of the play that George and Martha's cruelty to each other and to their guests is at its most vicious and hurtful.

"The Exorcism" is a rite to rid a possessed person of the devil within him or her. Martha is the subject of an exorcism when George convinces her that their son—a figment of their imagination—is dead, that the illusion that has sustained them must be eliminated if they are going to face reality.

14. Gamesmanship is one of the play's major themes and is expressed in the title of the first act, "Fun and Games." Albee is emphasizing the games everyone plays in life, particularly those that are harmful to ourselves and to others. George and Martha's games have moved beyond the needs of a normal couple to chide each other for their faults. They now are capable of wounding each other deeply as these games have become a substitute for real communication between them. In the play, their need to lash out extends to include Nick and Honey; and the party games, including "Humiliate the Host," "Get the Guests," "Bringing Up Baby," etc. (as named by George), provide the framework for their marital battles. George's decision to "kill" his and Martha's son provides the climactic game that may change their lives forever.

15. To answer this question, you must look for evidence within the play to support your feelings about Albee's intentions. If you feel George and Martha are better off for having rid themselves of the illusion that they have a son, then you might compare the characters at the beginning of the play and at the end to show a progression. If you feel the ending of the play suggests hopelessness, you might look to the traditions of the Theater of the Absurd (and to Albee's other plays) to suggest the feelings of futility common to this movement among dramatists. In either case, your answer will probably be subjective, but be sure to back up your opinions with solid evidence from the play.

Test 2

1. A	**2.** C	**3.** C	**4.** A	**5.** B	**6.** A
7. A	**8.** A	**9.** B	**10.** B		

11. On one level, Nick and Honey are necessary to the play because they provide an audience for George and Martha's verbal battles. George and Martha need spectators for their games to be truly effective, and this time the audience happens to be Nick and Honey. The younger couple also represent the play's real audience; that is, they act as stand-ins for our own shock and embarrassment as we watch George and Martha tear each other apart. On a thematic level, Nick and Honey are a contrast to George and Martha. Nick is on the way up; George is a failure. Martha is loud and aggressive; Honey is pallid and weak. George is a historian; Nick, a biologist. Martha can't have children; Honey uses secret means of birth control. Finally, however sad the outcome, George and Martha attempt to communicate with each other; Nick and Honey seem destined never to connect.

12. At first, the song (an academic parody of "Who's Afraid of the Big Bad Wolf?") is a party joke, an intellectual game song heard at Martha's father's party. In the first act, the four characters discuss its merits as a laugh-getter. At the end of the first act, George repeats the song in order to drown out one of Martha's bitter denunciations of him. He sings it again in Act II to cover up his knowledge that Martha and Nick are about to have sex with each other. And by the end of the play George is singing the song as a lullaby to soothe Martha after the devastation of the "death" of their son. Albee has said that the song means "Who's afraid to live life without illusions?"—that is, who's afraid to face reality? Martha's confession that she's "afraid of Virginia Woolf" is an admission that she's frightened of, and vulnerable to, reality and of what the future holds for her.

13. Three of the characters are revealed to have troubled relationships with their parents. Martha's father is a

powerful man in the college. She worships him, but, according to George, her father doesn't return her love. There is the suggestion that Martha has looked for a father substitute in marrying George and hates him for not living up to the older man's image. George tells the story of a young boy who murdered his mother and was responsible for his father's death. Whether or not the story is true, it reveals a deep-seated parental hatred on George's part. Honey's father was a corrupt preacher who may have stolen money from the church. Both Martha and Honey are failed parents: Martha has created an imaginary child to take the place of the one she couldn't have, and Honey, after one false pregnancy, has secretly used birth control to counteract her deep fear of childbirth. Also, Martha is seen ironically as an "earth mother," fertile and sexual; Honey is portrayed as the eternal child, prone to sickness and curled up like a baby in the womb on the bathroom floor.

14. The imaginary child is important to the play for several reasons. On one level, it gives the play suspense, as the audience wonders why George is so insistent that the subject of the child not be mentioned. On a symbolic level, the child represents George and Martha's need to share something private amid the wreck of their marriage, even an illusion, since the thought of facing the reality of their lives is too painful. Another possibility is that the child represents the sterility of American lives, in which the dream of the perfect child is merely an illusion, impossible to achieve in a world of adultery, alcoholism, lying, and evasion. Finally, the child acts as the catalyst in George's last gesture against Martha, a gesture both sadistic and healing. His decision to "kill" the child results in Martha's realization that reality must be faced, whatever the consequences. And the consequences for both George and Martha are, at best, uncertain.

15. At the beginning, Nick and Honey seem like the perfect all-American couple—young, attractive, on their way to success. As the play progresses, a different couple emerges. Nick reveals himself to be coldhearted and a bit ruthless, ready to do whatever it takes to get to the top. Honey seems silly and hopelessly inane until she reveals herself to be deeply frightened of reality, an eternal child who refuses to grow up to the responsibilities of life (as represented by childbirth). Nick comprehends George and Martha's secret, but whether he is changed by it is a question the play doesn't answer. As Martha is describing her son, Honey cries out that she wants a child, but Honey's future is ambiguous, too. Whether she will feel the same way after she has sobered up is never clarified.

Term Paper Ideas
and other
Topics for Writing

The Play

1. Discuss the influence of the Theater of the Absurd on *Who's Afraid of Virginia Woolf?*

2. In what way is *Who's Afraid of Virginia Woolf?* a departure from the realistic tradition of Eugene O'Neill and Tennessee Williams? In what way is it similar?

3. Are the issues presented in *Who's Afraid of Virginia Woolf?* still vital? Explain.

4. Compare Albee's view of the world in *Who's Afraid of Virginia Woolf?* with that in his play *A Delicate Balance*.

5. Is *Who's Afraid of Virginia Woolf?* a hopeful play? A pessimistic one? Explain.

6. The lost or nonexistent child has appeared in other plays by Edward Albee. Compare the roles in the other plays with the role of the imaginary child in *Who's Afraid of Virginia Woolf?*

7. It has been said that *Who's Afraid of Virginia Woolf?* is concerned with "salvaging, not savaging" a relationship. Do you agree or disagree? Explain.

Characters

1. Is George a hero or a villain in the play? Explain.

2. In what ways are George and Martha alike? In what ways different?

3. Does *Who's Afraid of Virginia Woolf?* have a main character? Who is it? Defend your answer.

4. Compare the characters of Nick and George, and of Martha and Honey.

5. How does the character of Martha's father influence the play?

6. In what ways are George and Martha likable characters?

7. Discuss the function of Nick and Honey in the play.

8. In what ways are George and Martha allegorical figures?

Themes

1. In what way does sex function in *Who's Afraid of Virginia Woolf?*

2. Compare the theme of truth and illusion in *Who's Afraid of Virginia Woolf?* and Tennessee Williams's *A Streetcar Named Desire.*

3. Discuss the theme of revenge in the play. What characters are bent on revenge, and why? How do you think Albee regards revenge?

Literary Topics

1. In what ways is *Who's Afraid of Virginia Woolf?* a comedy? Explain.

2. Describe the ways in which the past affects the present in the lives of the four characters.

3. In what ways is Albee's dialogue realistic? In what ways is it not? Give examples.

4. Discuss Albee's use of maxims, metaphors, puns, and humor. Give examples.

5. Explain what is meant by dark comedy and how *Who's Afraid of Virginia Woolf?* fits into this category of drama.

Theatrical Topics

1. What qualities would you look for if you were casting the four characters of this play?

2. Research three or four contemporary theatrical reviews of the play. Explain why you agree or disagree with their judgments of the play.

Further Reading
CRITICAL WORKS

Amacher, Richard E. *Edward Albee.* Boston: Twayne, 1982. Good overview of Albee's work through *The Lady from Dubuque.*

Bigsby, C. W. E. *Albee*. Edinburgh: Oliver and Boyd, 1969. Discussion of Albee's work up to *A Delicate Balance*.

Clurman, Harold. *The Naked Image: Observations on the Modern Theater*. New York: Macmillan, 1966. Includes a perceptive essay on *Who's Afraid of Virginia Woolf?*

Diehl, Digby. "Edward Albee Interviewed." *Transatlantic Review* 13 (Summer 1963): 57–72.

Esslin, Martin. *The Theater of the Absurd*. Garden City, N.Y.: Doubleday, 1969. The best book to read to learn about Albee's place in this movement.

Hayman, Ronald. *Edward Albee*. New York: Frederick Ungar, 1973. A British writer offers a view of Albee's work.

Meyer, Ruth. "Language: Truth and Illusion in *Who's Afraid of Virginia Woolf?*" *Education Theatre Journal* 20 (1968): 60–69.

Paolucci, Anne. *From Tension to Tonic: The Plays of Edward Albee*. Carbondale: Southern Illinois University, 1972. Cogent look at Albee's work.

Rutenberg, Michael. *Edward Albee: Playwright in Protest*. New York: Drama Book Specialists, 1969. The writer brings a critical eye to and a director's perspective on the plays.

Schechner, Richard. "Who's Afraid of Edward Albee?" *Tulane Drama Review* 7, no. 3 (1963): 7–10. Read this critical blast along with the next two entries in this list.

———. "Reality Is Not Enough: An Interview with Alan Schneider." *Tulane Drama Review* 9, no. 3 (1965): 143–50. One of the play's foes speaks with its Broadway director.

Schneider, Alan. "Why So Afraid?" *Tulane Drama Review* 7, no. 3 (1963): 10–13. The director responds to

Schechner's attack. This article, along with the preceding two entries on this list will give you a good idea of the controversy surrounding the play when it was first performed.

Stenz, Anita Maria. *Edward Albee: The Poet of Loss.* New York: Mouton, 1978.

Trilling, Diana. "The Riddle of Albee's *Who's Afraid of Virginia Woolf?*" In *Claremont Essays.* New York: Harcourt Brace, 1963. The author speaks to the play's enormous popularity.

Wasserman, Julian N. *Edward Albee: An Interview and Essays.* Houston, Tex.: The University of St. Thomas, 1983. One of Albee's most recent interviews.

AUTHOR'S OTHER WORKS

The dates in this list refer to composition not first performance.

1958	*The Zoo Story* (one act)
1959	*The Death of Bessie Smith* (one act)
1959	*The Sandbox* (one act)
1960	*The American Dream* (one act)
1963	*The Ballad of the Sad Cafe*
1964	*Tiny Alice*
1965	*Malcolm*
1966	*A Delicate Balance*
1967	*Everything in the Garden*
1968	*Box* and *Quotations from Chairman Mao Tse-Tung*
1971	*All Over*
1975	*Seascape*
1975	*Listening* (one act)
1976	*Counting the Ways* (one act)
1980	*The Lady from Dubuque*

1981   *Lolita*
1983   *The Man with Three Arms*

Glossary

Abstruse Hard to understand.

Alice Faye Blond film star of the 1940s, known for her musical roles.

"Bergin" Variation on *bourbon*, coined in the story George tells about a friend of his youth.

Bucolic Descriptive of an idealized rural life, shepherds, and farmland.

Chromosomes Threadlike bodies found in a human cell that carry the genes.

Clip joint Slang term for a bar or nightclub that overcharges its customers.

Daguerreotype Photo created by an obsolete photographic process using a silver plate. The process was invented by a French painter, Louis Daguerre (1789–1851).

Dies Irae Latin for Day of Wrath, name of a hymn on Judgment Day sung in requiem masses in the Roman Catholic church. George recites the *Dies Irae* as Martha describes their son during the "exorcism."

Exorcism Religious rite in which a person is freed from a demon that possesses the soul. Albee named the play's third act "The Exorcism" to suggest that Martha and George's imaginary child was such a demon.

Fen Swamp

Floozie Slang term for a gaudily dressed woman; a prostitute.

Frau German word for "wife."

Genes Chemical units that carry hereditary characteristics from parent to child.

Malleability Ability to be shaped or easily influenced.

New Carthage College town where George and Martha live, named after the North African state conquered by the Romans in the Punic Wars.

Pagan Heathen; a person with either primitive or no religious beliefs.

Peritonitis Disease where the lining of the abdomen is inflamed.

Prohibition Period from 1920 to 1933 when the sale of alcoholic beverages was forbidden in the United States.

Recondite Difficult to understand, obscure.

Requiem mass Mass said for the dead.

Theater of the Absurd Theatrical movement (loosely grouped and not formally organized) whose writers are characterized by a bleak and often hopeless view of the world, as well as a disregard for "standard" theatrical techniques to convey their messages. Albee is considerd to have been influenced by the Absurdists and to incorporate some of their techniques in his work.

Voyeur Person who gets sexual gratification from looking at the sexual actions of others.

Walpurgisnacht Literally "Witches' Night," a legendary rite taking place when witches gather for the purposes of evil and sexual wantonness. Albee named Act II of *Virginia Woolf* after this rite to suggest the wickedness engaged in by the characters.

Wanton Characterized by immoral behavior.

Woolf, Virginia British writer (1882–1941) known for her experiments in fictional technique. Her relationship to the play's title is indirect at best. That her

name is used in a parody song at an academic party
suggests more about the intellectual level of the characters than it does about her own writings or personal
life.

The Critics

On the Play

Without attempting to enthrone Albee alongside
anyone (though I personally admire him above all
other Americans now writing for the stage), or to
hail *Virginia Woolf* as a classic of the modern theatre
(which I have no doubt it will become), I would only
state that, in my experience, a more honest or moral
(in the true sense) playwright does not exist—un-
less it be Samuel Beckett . . . And if what Albee is
doing is giving us a "sentimentalized" view of ourselves rather than one as harshly and starkly un-
sentimental as any I know, why didn't those theatre
party ladies buy it up ahead of time as they do all
those other technicolor postcards which pass for
plays? Or is Albee not rather dedicated to smashing
that rosy view, shocking us with the truth of our
present-day behavior and thought, striving to purge
us into an actual confrontation with reality?
—*Alan Schneider*, "Why So
Afraid?" in Tulane Drama
Review, 1963

The upsetting thing—the deeply upsetting thing—
is that American theatre-goers and their critics have
welcomed this phony play and its writer as the har-
binger of a new wave in the American theatre. The
American theatre, our theatre, is so hungry, so vo-
racious, so corrupt, so morally blind, so perverse
that *Virginia Woolf* is a success. I am outraged at a
theatre and an audience that accepts as a masterpiece an insufferably long play with great preten-

sions that lacks intellectual size, emotional insight, and dramatic electricity. I'm tired of play-long "metaphors"—such as the illusory child of *Virginia Woolf*—which are neither philosophically, psychologically, nor poetically valid. I'm tired of plays that are badly plotted and turgidly written being excused by such palaver as "organic unity" or "inner form." I'm tired of morbidity and sexual perversity which are there only to titillate an impotent and homosexual theatre and audience. I'm tired of Albee.

> —*Richard Schechner*, "Who's Afraid of Edward Albee?" in Tulane Drama Review, *1963*

On Martha

The characterization of Martha is certainly proof of the author's understanding of the problems of unfulfilled people. The social conditioning which encouraged Martha's thwarted expectations, as well as George's idealism and her childlessness are all realities which contributed to her disappointment and sorrow. However, in spite of the material advantages with which she grew up, Martha, given her loveless childhood—not unlike Jerry in *The Zoo Story*—entered adult life as an emotional cripple who doubted her worth as a human being. She did nothing constructive to help herself to make life bearable for George or for herself . . . The residue of her wasted talents and unused energies are released in the form of abusive behavior toward her husband. Her pain makes her ruthlessly egotistical. Fairly considered against her given background, there should be little room for complacency or self-righteousness in an evaluation of this character. If her selfishness and cruelty make her repugnant, her deep unhappiness and almost dumb suffering should arouse compassion.

> —*Anita M. Stenz*, Edward Albee: The Poet of Loss, *1978*

On George

Whatever the truth about his past really is, George worked it out creatively in the form of a novel. The tragic story of a boy who accidently [sic] shot his mother and then a year later while trying to avoid hitting a porcupine on the road swerved the car and drove his father into a tree. Commentators have interpreted what they perceive as George's withdrawal and passivity as behavior resulting from his responsibility as an adolescent for the death of both parents. More in keeping with the play, whose key phrase spoken throughout by both George and Martha is "Truth and illusion, don't you know the difference?", is the theory that George's killing of his parents is symbolic but that there is real guilt attached to his need to be cruel. This also explains why George waited until it was almost too late before he was able to bring himself to hurt Martha and himself profoundly enough to free them both from the mutually destructive pattern of their married life.

—*Anita M. Stenz*, Edward Albee:
The Poet of Loss, *1978*

On George and Martha

Albee has succeeded in persuading us that Martha, as well as George, is a genuinely pitiable character. Thus one can say that the plot contains a kind of reversal, for while Martha had the upper hand over him in her role of his antagonist during the first two acts, he now has won at the fun-and-games business—but at so considerable a cost as to amount to only a pyrrhic victory. At least, however, they communicate, understand each other, and are together at the curtain. They are nevertheless so weakened by the strain of the exorcism and by the bleak prospect that lies before them that we can only pity both of them. It seems to me that we see in them something of the whole general problem of humanity suffering from forces beyond its control, forces which lie inside us as well as outside us and which make us fearful when we recognize them. Martha's fear, then, is exactly the right note for the terminal effect of this highly indeterminate ending.

—*Richard E. Amacher*, Edward Albee, *1982*

On the Imaginary Child

When George and Martha destroy that child they destroy whatever illusions they have created in reaction to a reality that has been responsible for the loneliness they feel. And the reality they try to keep away, by conjuring up a fantasy child, is actually the reality of man's predicament. That is, man—in this very complex and bureaucratic world whose sheer organization is dehumanizing—feels an overwhelming sense of aloneness and separation. His inability to deal effectively with this predicament has left him filled with despair and boredom, for he no longer has the joy of individual creativity, only dependency on an outside power. And when he can no longer create, he begins to destroy, because either activity lifts him out of his insignificance. George and Martha feel this dislocation, almost abandonment, brought on by our modern world—only more so because their marriage is sterile. Consequently, in order to overcome their predicament, they have resorted to the illusion that they are not alone; they have a child who loves them.

—*Michael Rutenberg*, Edward Albee: Playwright in Protest, *1969*

On Nick and Honey

Nick and Honey are just starting out and have something of the hopes and energies that George and Martha had when they first came together; but where George failed, Nick might well succeed. He is willful in a petty way, knows exactly what he wants, and is callous enough to reach out and grab it. His plans are clear and realizable. He is much more practical and less idealistic than George, but lacks George's potential to adjust to what the world calls failure. George's *failure* is incomprehensible to Nick: would anyone, in his right mind, turn down a high administrative post simply to indulge a passion to write the great American novel? The irony is that Nick wants what George had in his grasp and turned down. In this context, Nick's designs seem downright petty, while George's worldly failure takes on heroic colors . . . [Nick] is absolutely callous to [Honey's] emotional needs, bent on humoring her in order to get what he wants. His relationship with Honey is an excellent barometer of his relationship with the rest of the world. He will very likely get everything he wants; but the world will hold his success against him, for his ambition is utterly transparent. George and Martha have understood this and are contemptuous of him; Honey suspects it but cannot bring herself to face the truth.

—*Anne Paolucci*, From Tension to
Tonic, 1972

NOTES

NOTES

LaVergne, TN USA
21 March 2011
220936LV00001B/143/A